Divine Worship
by John Corbet (1620-1680)
with chapters by C. Matthew McMahon

Copyright Information

Divine Worship, by John Corbet, with chapters by C. Matthew McMahon
Edited by Therese B. McMahon

Copyright ©2025 by Puritan Publications and A Puritan's Mind™

Some language and grammar have been updated from the original manuscript. Any change in wording or punctuation has not changed the intent or meaning of the original authors, and has been made to aid the modern reader.

Published by Puritan Publications
A Ministry of A Puritan's Mind™ in Crossville, TN.
www.apuritansmind.com
www.puritanpublications.com

All rights reserved. No part of this publication may be reproduced, stored in a retrieval system or transmitted in any form by any means, electronic, mechanical, photocopy, recording or otherwise, without the prior permission of the publisher, except as provided by USA copyright law.

This Print Edition, 2025
Electronic Edition, 2025
Manufactured in the United States of America

ISBN: 978-1-62663-529-6
eISBN: 978-1-62663-528-9

Table of Contents

Meet John Corbet 7

Introduction 12

Preface to the Reader 18

The First Part: Worship 20

    §1. Concerning Worship in General 20

    §2. Concerning Divine Worship in Its Broader Sense 20

    §3. Concerning Divine Worship in Its Stricter Sense, Which Is Chiefly Intended Here 21

    §4. Divine Worship Distinguished into Internal and External 22

    §5. Divine Worship Distinguished into Natural and Instituted; and First, Concerning Natural Worship 24

    §6. Concerning Divine Instituted Worship 25

    §7. Concerning Moral and Ceremonial Worship 26

    §8. The Parts of Worship Distinguished from Their Adjuncts or Accidents 28

    §9. Concerning Those Acts of Religion That Are Moral Natural Worship 30

    §10. Concerning Particular Acts Which Are Natural Ceremonial Worship 32

    §11. Concerning External Acts Which, by the Custom of the Age or Country, Express Devotion in Worship 34

Table of Contents

§12. Concerning External Acts Which, by Divine Institution or General Custom of Nations, Express Divine Honor 35

§13. Concerning Fasting, Wearing of Sackcloth or Mean Apparel, Lying in Ashes, Going Barefoot, and Other Austerities Used in God's Worship 36

§14. Concerning the Nature of Monastic Vows of Obedience, Poverty, and Chastity 38

§15. Concerning Decency and Order as Adjuncts of Divine Worship 39

§16. Concerning Time and Place Considered as Adjuncts or as Matter of Worship 41

§17. Concerning Sacred Signs and Significant Ceremonies in Divine Worship 44

§18. Concerning the Nature of Holiness and the Distinctions of Holiness 45

The Second Part: Idolatry 50

§1. Concerning Superstition in General 50

§2. Concerning Idolatry in General 52

§3. Concerning *Latria* and *Dulia* 53

§4. Concerning Idolatry, Serious and Dissembled 55

§5. Concerning Adoration Given to the Host 57

§6. Concerning the Popish Invocation of Angels and Departed Saints 59

§7. Concerning the Erecting of Altars and the Bringing of Oblations to Any Besides God 63

§8. Concerning Making Vows to Any Besides God 64

§9. Concerning Burning Incense to Any Besides God...67

§10. Concerning the Dedicating of Places and Times, and the Erecting of Symbolical Presence to Any Besides God..67

§11. Concerning the Worship of Relics 69

§12. Concerning the Worship of the Cross............70

§13. Whether Christ as Man, or Mediator, is to be Worshipped... 71

§14. Of Worshipping Images, or of Idolatry in the Mediate Object of Worship 74

§15. Of the Worshipping of False Gods in Images 77

§16. Of Making Images of the True God 78

§17. Of Worshipping the True God in Images 81

§18. Of Material Images and Representations Not of God, but of Other Things Used in God's Worship, and of the Symbols of the Divine Presence; of Worshipping Towards the East, and Bowing Towards the Altar 82

§19. Of the Scandalous Use of Images.....................86

§20. Of the Mere Appearance of Idolatry in Any Kind...87

§21. Whether a Course of Idolatry in What Kind Soever Infer a State of Damnation 88

The Third Part: Superstition 91

§1. Of Excess in the Quantity or Measure of Religious Observances...91

Table of Contents

§2. Of Excess in Religious Observances, for the Kind Thereof 92

§3. Of the Rule that Limits the Kinds of Worship 92

§4. What of Divine Worship May Not be Devised or Instituted by Man 95

§5. What Things Pertaining to Divine Worship May be Devised or Instituted by Man 97

§6. Concerning the Lawfulness of Significant Ceremonies in Divine Worship 100

§7. Concerning bowing at the Name of Jesus 105

§8. Concerning Kneeling in the Sacrament 106

§9. Concerning Wearing the Surplice 106

§10. Concerning the Ring in Matrimony 108

§11. Concerning the Cross in Baptism 108

§12. Concerning Holy-days 110

§13. Concerning a Liturgy 113

§14. Concerning Religious Austerities, as Acts or Matter of Divine Worship 113

Other Works at Puritan Publications on Worship 116

Meet John Corbet
Edited by C. Matthew McMahon, Ph.D., Th.D.

John Corbet (1620–1680) was a preacher forged in the flames of England's great convulsions. Born in Gloucester, the son of Roger Corbet, a humble shoemaker, he came up through the grammar school of that city and entered Magdalen Hall, Oxford, in 1636. There he earned his Bachelor of Arts on January 5, 1639. It was not long before the fire of ministry took hold of him. Ordained soon after, he was appointed to serve at St. Mary-de-Crypt in Gloucester, not only as a city lecturer, but also as usher to the free school tied to his church.

When the Parliament garrisoned Gloucester during the Civil War, Corbet stood fast in the pulpit as chaplain to Colonel Edward Massey, the city's governor. He preached boldly against the crown, declaring without flinch that "nothing had so much deceived the world as the name of a king, which was the ground of all mischief to the church of Christ." His alignment with Massey gave him firsthand knowledge of military affairs, and his account of the siege and the conduct of the war up to June 1643, written in plain speech and without commentary, has stood as a vital record of those days.

With the war behind him, Corbet labored in Bridgwater, Somerset, and later in Chichester. He was then installed at the rectory of Bramshot in Hampshire, and while in that charge, he sought the degree of

Bachelor of Divinity on May 14, 1658. Whether the degree was ever granted, none can say.

The year 1662 brought down the storm of nonconformity. Corbet was cast out of Bramshot under the Act of Uniformity, and he withdrew to London. He lived quietly, preaching not, until the death of his first wife—whose name and story remain hidden. In time he entered the home of Sir John Micklethwaite, President of the College of Physicians, and later made his abode with Alderman Webb of Totteridge in Hertfordshire, that he might live close to his friend Richard Baxter.

His second marriage bound him to a daughter of Dr. William Twiss, the renowned divine. He joined Baxter's household, where, as Baxter himself testified, they never disagreed in doctrine, worship, or polity—whether civil or ecclesiastical—nor exchanged one displeasing word.

When King Charles II published his license for religious assemblies in March 1671, some of Corbet's former flock called him back to Chichester. While dwelling there, he took part in a public disputation with Bishop Gunning and the Church of England clergy. The bishop, by some accounts, handled Corbet unjustly and with contempt. Yet, even while racked by the torment of kidney stones, Corbet continued to preach until November 1680. Seeking relief, he returned to London, but died on December 26th before any surgical aid could be given. He was buried at St. Andrew's, Holborn.

His funeral sermon was delivered by Richard Baxter, who honored him as a man "so blameless in all his conversation," that none ever accused him but for nonconformity.

The works of John Corbet are:
1. *A Historicall Relation of the Military Government of Gloucester from the beginning of the Civill Warre betweene the King and the Parliament, to the recall of Colonell Massie* (1645, 4to); later reissued as *A True and Impartiall Historie of the Military Government* (1647, 4to), and also included in *Somers Tracts*, vol. v., and in Washbourn's *Bibliotheca Gloucestrensis*, pp. 1–152.
2. *A Vindication of the Magistrates of the City of Gloucester from the Calumnies of Robert Bacon* (1646, 4to).
3. *Ten Questions Discussed*, a rebuke of Antinomian errors.
4. *The Interest of England in the Matter of Religion* (1661, 8vo, 2 parts). This drew sharp responses from Sir Roger L'Estrange in *Interest Mistaken, or the Holy Cheat* (1661), and later from the anonymous authors of *Presbyterian Unmasked* (1676, 1681). Baxter lamented how a nameless pen vented a "bloody invective" against Corbet's peaceable tract, accusing him as though he intended to stir up war (*Works*, xviii. 188).

5. *A Discourse of the Religion of England* (1667, 4to), answered the same year in *A Discourse of Toleration*, anonymously published but attributed to Dr. Perinchief, prebendary of Westminster.
6. *A Second Discourse of the Religion of England* (1668, 4to), which likewise met with reply.
7. *The Kingdom of God among Men* (1679, 8vo).
8. *A Point of Church Unity Discussed.*
9. *An Account of Himself about Conformity.*
10. *Self-employment in Secret* (1681, 12mo), published posthumously in 1700, and many editions thereafter.
11. *The Nonconformist's Plea for Lay Communion with the Church of England,* together with *A Defence of My Endeavours for the Ministry,* written in response to Bishop Gunning (1683, 4to).
12. *A Humble Endeavour of Explication of the Operations of God* (1683, 4to).
13. Corbet's *Remains* (1684, 4to).

He also contributed to the first volume of Rushworth's *Historical Collections*.

For further reading:
Wood's *Fasti*, vol. i, p. 507; *Athenae Oxonienses* (Bliss), vol. iii, p. 1264; Baxter's *Works* (Orme edition), vol. xviii, pp.

Divine Worship

162–192; Palmer's *Nonconformist's Memorial*, vol. ii, p. 259; and Washbourn's *Bibliotheca Gloucestrensis*, vol. i,

Introduction
by C. Matthew McMahon, Ph.D., Th.D.

There are few doctrines more neglected in our generation and few words more misused than "worship." The modern church, ever chasing its own tail, sings louder, dances longer, and builds higher stages—yet all the while digs itself deeper into ignorance doing what God has never instructed (even more so, going back to Old Testament worship!). What was once a trembling reverence before the eternal God in ages past has been replaced by a fog machine and a ten-dollar coffee. If the saints of old could rise from the grave, they would not recognize what passes for *sacred*. (Can the modern church even define that word?) And if they could speak, they would thunder: "This is *not* worship." It is precisely here that the sober and God-fearing voice of John Corbet must be heard again.

Corbet was no fringe malcontent, nor was he the sort of man to fill his pages with anecdote and sentiment. He was a careful theologian, possessed of a conscience instructed by the Word and a heart pierced by the fear of God. In *Divine Worship*, he turns his full attention to the right manner of approaching the Majesty on high—not with flippant ritual nor with blind custom, but "with reverence and godly fear" (Hebrews 12:28). In an age where men bow their heads with mouths full of laughter and hearts full of self,

Corbet calls us back to the altar of sobriety, where God alone is great.

The work is divided into three parts. The first concerns itself with the *nature of worship*: what it is, to whom it belongs, in what ways it is rightly rendered. Here Corbet makes his definitions precise, slicing through muddled piety, like a farmer hacks down overgrowth with a sharp scythe. Worship, he shows, is not a matter of sincerity alone—pagans are often sincere—but must be rendered according to *divine prescription*. Cain learned this too late, Nadab and Abihu not at all.

Corbet distinguishes between internal and external worship, natural and instituted, moral and ceremonial, and reminds the reader—again and again—that worship is not a play of human invention. It is not *ours* to shape. God has not abdicated His right to *define* how He is honored. To worship the true God with false means is no better than worshiping a false god altogether. "In vain do they worship me, teaching for doctrines the commandments of men," (Matthew 15:9). These are not merely textual embellishments—they are judgments. The smoke that rises from unsanctioned altars is a stench in the Lord's nostrils.

The second part enters the thornier ground of ceremonial observances. Here, Corbet proceeds with cautious boldness. He does not light matches near barrels of powder, but neither does he tiptoe as if truth were breakable. Whether the matter be the sign of the cross in baptism, the kneeling at the Lord's Table, or the wearing of surplices—Corbet weighs each in the scale of Scripture and finds things wanting. He does not declare war on ceremony *per se*, but on superstition masquerading as faith. The issue, always, is whether God has appointed a thing—or whether man, in presumption, has *presumed* to *improve* upon the mind of God.

Ceremonial excess is not the invention of Antichrist in Rome alone; it is the product of human nature. Ever since Aaron crafted a golden calf and called it "a feast to the LORD," men have adorned their idolatry with biblical words. Corbet saw this creeping thing slithering through the Church of England—excesses in posture, garb, and gesture that threatened to swallow up the simplicity of the Gospel. He does not strike with wild fists but rather with a theologian's scalpel. It is not the bowing of the knee that he objects to, but the making of such bowing a binding ordinance. It is not the surplice that troubles him, but the pharisaical spirit that adorns itself in white linen while the heart remains defiled.

To the modern reader, some of these matters may appear *quaint*—after all, who today argues over the wearing of linen? But the underlying disease has not changed, only its symptoms. What once adorned altars now shines on stages. What was once muttered in Latin is now shouted in "worship ditties" and *pop anthems*. The same soul-dead ritualism thrives, now baptized in relevance. Corbet's analysis is not antiquated—it is prophetic.

The third part of *Divine Worship* turns to excesses in the acts of religion themselves—where the measure or kind of religious observance outruns the bounds of Scripture. Here Corbet targets the more subtle shades of superstition: praying too long, preaching without season, fasting to impress men, holy-days made holier than the Lord's Day itself. He is no enemy of reverence, but a surgeon of excess. "God is not the author of confusion, but of peace," (1 Corinthians 14:33), and Corbet aims to disentangle devotion from the vines of vanity.

It is here that his pastoral sense shines. He does not rail against earnest Christians but warns them. He does not dismantle piety, but refines it. He understands that religious people often err not from malice but from zeal without knowledge. Like Uzzah, they reach out to steady the ark with good intent and fall dead for lack of command. "Obedience is better than sacrifice," (1 Samuel 15:22), and Corbet labors to prove it.

He also speaks, perhaps more clearly than most of his contemporaries, to the relationship between Christian liberty and ecclesiastical power. On matters such as kneeling, wearing the surplice, or using a ring in marriage, Corbet draws careful lines. If these are indifferent in themselves, they must not be imposed. And if they are imposed in a way that scandalizes the weak or binds the conscience, they cease to be indifferent. This is not just solving moral problems. It is biblical charity guided by confessional integrity. His judgments are not arbitrary—they are shepherdly.

What emerges from all three parts is a singular, weighty truth: *God is to be worshiped in the way He has commanded, not in the way man finds convenient, beautiful, or ancient.* The Reformation was not fought merely over justification but over *worship*. Antichristian Rome did not err only in its doctrine of grace but in its glut of inventions at the altar. Corbet understood this. He did not pick at symptoms—he severed the root. And the root of all superstition is this: man believing himself wiser than God.

Modern Evangelicals, (yes, modern *so-called* Reformed denominations too) if they are to benefit from Corbet's work, must repent of the aesthetic addiction that now governs worship. They must learn to ask not "Does it feel sincere?" but "Has God required it?" They must stop speaking of worship as if it were a *concert* or a *catharsis*. Until the church recovers the regulative principle—not in mere word but in actual practice—the modern church shall go on building churches that entertain goats and starve sheep. Corbet offers no such amusement. He calls us to tremble.

His work is not a handbook for liturgical minimalists, nor a tract for narrow partisans. It is the sober cry of a minister who feared God more than man, and who loved Christ more than *church speakers* and *church fashion*. He stands among those rare and steady voices—Watson, Owen, Perkins—who looked into the Scriptures not to decorate themselves but to humble themselves. And from that humble place, they wrote.

Divine Worship deserves its name. It reminds us that the God we worship is not our equal, nor our partner, nor our guest. He is the Lord of hosts, before whom angels veil their faces and elders fall down. He is a consuming fire. And He will be worshiped—not on our terms, but on His.

May the reader approach Corbet's work with solemnness, *seriousness*. Not as a historical curiosity, but as a cry from the wall: "See what God has said. See what man has done. And tremble." For if we would honor God rightly, we must first learn to fear Him rightly. And Corbet will teach us both.

In Christ's grace and mercy,
C. Matthew McMahon, Ph.D., Th.D.
From My study, June, 2025
"...search the Scriptures..." (John 5:39).
www.apuritansmind.com
www.puritanpublications.com
www.gracechapeltn.com
www.reformedsynod.com

Preface to the Reader

It has seemed necessary to me, both as a Christian and a minister—and as one who has suffered for conscientious hesitation and disagreement concerning certain parts of worship commanded by authority—to search diligently into the nature of Divine Worship. What I have discerned in this weighty subject, through God's gracious help in reading and reflection, I have attempted to set down briefly here. I have done so in order to have a clear summary of my thoughts on the matter, close at hand, for correction where I have erred, for refinement where I am right, and for easier use whenever occasion demands. I have also written this with the hope that others, who will take the trouble to read and reflect upon it, might aid me toward a fuller and clearer understanding of these things. I am well aware of my shortcomings in this knowledge and desire, with humility, to grow in clarity and precision. Yet I am not uncertain about the chief points of divine worship.

In the body of a living creature, the larger veins are easily traced throughout their course; the smaller ones, with more difficulty; and the smallest are nearly invisible. So it is in theology: the larger veins—the most essential and weighty truths—are plainly seen and cannot be mistaken. But the smaller branches are less easily identified and cannot be followed in all their turns without careful and exact inquiry. Every man ought to strive for as clear an understanding as he can attain in the matters that pertain to his calling and practice. Still, when we have done all, we know only in part and see through a glass, darkly (1 Corinthians 13:12). This awareness ought to produce in those of differing opinions a spirit of thoughtfulness and sobriety, such that one does not despise or condemn another, but all receive one another in mutual love.

JOHN CORBET

The First Part: Worship

§1. Concerning Worship in General

Regarding worship in general, some define it as an observance given to others in accordance with their excellence or worthiness. In this broad sense, it is essentially the same as giving honor. Thus, worship in this way may be given not only to superiors, but also to equals and even inferiors, based on whatever natural, moral, or political worth they may possess, in line with the Apostle's command: "Honour all men" (1 Peter 2:17).

However, others give the concept of worship a more narrow definition than that of honor. And rightly so, I believe. They define it as a particular kind of regard—not simply based on someone's excellence or worth, but specifically on their superiority and authority over us, whether that be in nature, civil standing, or church office—and such regard includes an act of subjection.

The highest kind of worship is that which belongs to the highest excellency and authority, and this is what we call *Divine Worship*.

§2. Concerning Divine Worship in Its Broader Sense

To worship God is to give Him that observance which is due to Him alone, based on His incommunicable excellence, His sovereignty over us, and His other superior relations to us.

The observance that is due to God alone is our voluntary act of absolute, unlimited subjection to Him, and everything that expresses such subjection. All acts of divine worship are rooted in this, and therefore, by their very nature, must be the highest kind of observance that can be rendered. Yet within this category, there are multiple kinds or parts that vary in how fully they partake of this highest kind. Some partake of it in a more noble and excellent way, while others in a lower way—yet these lower acts support and serve the higher.

Every act of obedience to God, when viewed formally as obedience, is divine worship in a *broad* sense. For such obedience directly gives to God the honor and observance He is due. Therefore, devotion to God encompasses the whole duty of man; for man's entire duty goes no further than what is owed to God.

Still, those acts which belong to our duty toward God, but which are immediately directed toward our neighbor or ourselves, are not in themselves directly religious or divine worship. Rather, they are so in a secondary sense—as they are commanded by religion.

§3. Concerning Divine Worship in Its Stricter Sense, Which Is Chiefly Intended Here

To worship God is to directly acknowledge His being, His attributes, and His sovereignty over us, and to do so for His honor. It is to render unto Him the kind of honor that cannot be given to any other, because His being, His perfections, and His supreme relations to us are incommunicable.

Therefore, it is not a proper or meaningful question—because there is no room for debate—whether divine worship may be given to a creature. The real question, when some give worship to a creature, is whether the worship they offer is in fact divine worship, that which rightly belongs to God. And if it is, then it is immediately clear that it cannot rightly be given to any creature. For the worship that belongs to God is as incommunicable as His excellence.

But to answer the question as it is commonly phrased—whether religious worship may be given to a creature—one must distinguish between the elicited acts of religion and the commanded acts of religion. That religious worship, in the sense of commanded acts, may be shown to men, is not in dispute—for all proper civil observance is governed by the principles of religion. However, the elicited acts of religion—those which are acts of devotion offered to God as God—cannot be given to any creature, nor may any outward, commanded act that immediately expresses such devotion be given to a creature.

§4. Divine Worship Distinguished into Internal and External

All kinds of worship—including the worship of God—are divided into *internal* and *external*, corresponding to the essential parts of man: the soul and the body.

The *internal* worship of God is an act of the mind or soul, whereby, in light of God's worthiness, the soul holds a fitting estimation of Him, takes delight in Him, and consents to the appropriate expressions of that esteem. Clearly, the most essential and deepest part of divine worship is a supreme reverence for God and love toward Him (Deuteronomy 6:5: "And thou shalt love the Lord thy God with all thine heart, and with all thy soul, and with all thy might,").

The *external* worship of God is the direct and immediate expression of that inward esteem, through any outward sign, speech, or gesture in action.

Internal worship is to external worship as the soul is to the body. In fact, internal worship may stand alone as complete, especially when outward expression is either impossible or unnecessary.

External worship without the internal is like a lifeless body—form without substance. Still, such outward observance retains the nature of worship and carries moral weight or account before others (Isaiah 29:13, "Wherefore the Lord said, Forasmuch as this people draw near me with their mouth, and with their lips do honour me, but have removed their heart far from me...").

§5. Divine Worship Distinguished into Natural and Instituted; and First, Concerning Natural Worship

The worship of God is either natural or instituted. *Natural worship* is that which, in its kind and directly, is founded on the nature of God, the nature of man, God's relation to man, and man's relation to God.

This natural worship is of *two* types: that which is naturally necessary, and that which is naturally commendable. The first is essential and cannot be changed or dismissed. The second is to be used whenever fitting opportunity permits.

There is a kind of natural worship owed to God both as the Creator of man and as the Redeemer of fallen man. As our Creator, God is our absolute Possessor, Ruler, and Benefactor. Therefore, He is to be acknowledged by us with all appropriate reverence. Whatever acts of observance are due to God on this ground—because of His relation to us as our Creator—are natural worship.

All natural worship owed to God as Creator can be discerned through natural revelation, that is, through the Book of Nature (Romans 1:20: "For the invisible things of him from the creation of the world are clearly seen, being understood by the things that are made..."). In man's original state before the fall, such knowledge was fully and clearly accessible by nature. In the fallen state, it is seen more dimly and imperfectly—not because the evidences have changed, but because our faculties have become disordered and incapable of seeing them as we ought.

Likewise, there is a kind of worship naturally owed to God as our Redeemer—arising directly from the work of redemption and our new relation to Him through it. And this kind of worship—granted that redemption has taken place—is no more a matter of arbitrary institution than the worship grounded in the law of our original creation and innocence.

The knowledge of this kind of natural worship comes to us through the divine revelation by which we learn of our redeemed condition (2 Timothy 1:10: "But is now made manifest by the appearing of our Saviour Jesus Christ, who hath abolished death, and hath brought life and immortality to light through the gospel,"). But once that redemptive state is made known, reason itself will demonstrate that certain acts of reverence, in their specific form, are naturally and necessarily due to God as Redeemer.

§6. Concerning Divine Instituted Worship

Instituted worship is that which, in its specific form, depends directly on the free will of God and His sovereign appointment. However, once such an institution has been made and remains in force, it becomes necessarily and rightly owed to God—though it is not natural in its origin.

This is because our natural and unchanging relation to God obliges us always and *without exception* to do whatever He has ordained, to the extent and for as long as He has commanded it (Ecclesiastes 12:13: "Let us hear the conclusion of the whole matter: Fear God, and keep his commandments: for this is the whole duty of man,").

§7. Concerning Moral and Ceremonial Worship

This distinction, being commonly used, must be acknowledged here. It essentially overlaps with the previous distinction between natural and instituted worship. What is commonly referred to as *moral* worship is, for the most part—though not entirely—natural worship. Likewise, not all natural worship should necessarily be labeled *moral*, for there may be ceremonies that are natural in kind—that is, naturally commendable, though not absolutely required.

Furthermore, not all instituted worship is ceremonial. Some forms of instituted worship are moral in character, such as the observance of the weekly Sabbath, or the Lord's Day (Exodus 20:8: "Remember the sabbath day, to keep it holy,"). Likewise, not all ceremonial worship is instituted. In addition to naturally commendable ceremonies, there may be religious ceremonial acts that are used freely, on special occasions, and only once. These might be called *instituted* in the sense that they are not *natural*, but they are not instituted in the sense of being established or set as an ongoing rule.

The term *moral* itself is ambiguous and, in my judgment, not well-suited for this subject—just as it is also problematic when used to divide the divine law into *moral* and *ceremonial*. For every divine law is *moral* in the sense that it relates to our behavior (*circa mores*), and all acts of worship are moral in that they conform to God's law. Still, usage governs language, and we must accept the terminology commonly adopted, while seeking to understand what is meant by it.

Sometimes, those who use the word *moral* in this context mean that which is of perpetual obligation. But this cannot be its full meaning, since some things regarded as *moral* and not *ceremonial* are not perpetual. There is a recognized distinction between *moral natural* and *moral positive*. That *moral positive* duties are not perpetual by nature is beyond dispute. In fact, some *moral positive* duties are not perpetual in practice—such as the Sabbath on the seventh day. Though the physical rest of that day may have included ceremonial elements under the Mosaic law, yet the appointment of that day, and the setting apart of a fixed weekly period for solemn worship, was not ceremonial, nor natural, but *moral positive*. And yet it was not perpetual.

Moreover, there is nothing, in the nature of ceremonial laws or worship, that prevents God from making them permanent, if He so wills. In fact, there are ceremonial ordinances now in effect which shall endure until the end of the world—namely, the two sacraments of the New Testament (Matthew 28:19–20: "Go ye therefore, and teach all nations, baptizing them... teaching them to observe all things whatsoever I have commanded you: and, lo, I am with you alway, even unto the end of the world,").

The most useful terms I have found to express what is generally meant by *moral* and *ceremonial* worship are these: the former is *substantial*, and in itself an act of divine worship; the latter is *supplemental*—something attached to the former, helping to express and complete it outwardly. The word *complemental* might be appropriate here, except that it carries a misleading tone in common usage. Indeed, those who offer nothing but ceremonial worship to God do little more than *complement* Him, in the popular sense of that word.

Although ceremonial worship is only supplemental to that which is called *moral* or *substantial*, yet because it is appointed by God, it must not be taken lightly. It should be valued according to its weight and purpose. Some parts or forms of ceremonial worship are of great significance in religion—such as the sacraments and sacrifices under the Old Testament, and the sacraments under the New.

§8. The Parts of Worship Distinguished from Their Adjuncts or Accidents

Worship may be considered both as a general category and as a complete whole, and in each respect it has specific and integral parts. Every specific kind of worship contains within it the common designation and essence of the broader category. And every integral part within the same specific kind is uniform, sharing the same name and nature of that kind. However, parts that differ specifically from one another can also be seen as integral parts—though of diverse types—that together form a complete act of divine service.

It is of great importance to rightly recognize and distinguish between worship itself and those features which are only its adjuncts or accompanying elements—those things without which worship cannot be performed, or cannot be performed properly. These include things such as order, structure, choice of words, degree, frequency, time, place, and outward arrangements. These elements belong to worship, not in any uniquely religious sense, but in the same way that they pertain to any serious civil or human activity.

Moreover, these aspects do not immediately and directly concern God and His honor—who is the object of worship—but rather concern man and what is suitable for him, as the one performing the worship. Nevertheless, God and His honor are involved in them indirectly, because He is concerned that men approach Him with all fitting and appropriate circumstances. For this reason, such adjuncts ultimately relate to God and are to be used in the setting apart of His name as holy

(Leviticus 10:3, "I will be sanctified in them that come nigh me, and before all the people I will be glorified,").

I do not believe the proper way to distinguish worship from its adjuncts is to say that one part makes worship acceptable to God or is a means of grace, while the other does not. Both may serve these purposes, though not in the same *degree*.

Even though ceremonial worship is only an appendage to what is called moral or substantial worship, yet it is truly a distinct type of worship, because it shares in the general nature of worship. However, it is a species of worship in an analogical sense, possessing the essence of the category, but in a lower and subordinate way.

§9. Concerning Those Acts of Religion That Are Moral Natural Worship

The acts of religion that fall under the category of moral natural worship include the hearing of God's Word with a heart of submission (James 1:21, "Wherefore lay apart all filthiness and superfluity of naughtiness, and receive with meekness the engrafted word, which is able to save your souls,"); prayer, which encompasses the confession of our sin and misery (Psalm 32:5: "I acknowledged my sin unto thee, and mine iniquity have I not hid..."), petition for all necessary grace and mercy (Hebrews 4:16: "Let us therefore come boldly unto the throne of grace, that we may obtain mercy, and find grace to help in time of need,"), and praise with thanksgiving (Psalm 100:4: "Enter into his gates with thanksgiving, and into his courts with praise: be thankful unto him, and bless his name,").

Also included are self-resignation to God (Romans 12:1: "I beseech you therefore, brethren... that ye present your bodies a living sacrifice, holy, acceptable unto God, which is your reasonable service,"), entering into *covenant* with Him (Psalm 76:11: "Vow, and pay unto the Lord your God..."), making *vows* to Him, swearing by His name (Deuteronomy 10:20: "Thou shalt fear the Lord thy God; him shalt thou serve, and to him shalt thou cleave, and swear by his name,"), and dedicating anything for His immediate service (1 Samuel 1:28: "Therefore also I have lent him to the Lord; as long as he liveth he shall be lent to the Lord,").

All these are expressions of *divine honor*.

Each of these may also take on specific outward forms by positive institution, and in those forms they may be called *instituted worship*. Additionally, the thing vowed may be something instituted and ceremonial, though the act of making the vow itself is moral worship.

The purpose of an oath may be to confirm the truth before men (Hebrews 6:16: "For men verily swear by the greater: and an oath for confirmation is to them an end of all strife,"), and the immediate aim of a vow to God may result in some benefit to others. The content of a vow may also involve things that are ordinary. Yet, the vow in its essential nature is an act of divine worship—because it is a direct engagement made to God for His honor. Likewise, an oath, in its essential nature, is divine worship, because it directly acknowledges God's omnipotence, omniscience, and infinite holiness—calling Him to witness to the truth we affirm, and submitting ourselves voluntarily to His just judgment (Jeremiah 4:2: "And thou shalt swear, The Lord liveth, in truth, in judgment, and in righteousness...").

The internal purpose of both vow and oath is the glorifying of God as our Supreme Lord and Judge.

The external component of the sacraments, both in the Old and New Testament, constitutes instituted ceremonial worship. But the internal aspect—the soul and substance of the sacrament—being our solemn reception of the grace of the covenant given to us by God in Christ, and our solemn engagement to God in keeping with that covenant, is a highly important and essential part of divine service. This inward act is worship that is moral and natural.

§10. Concerning Particular Acts Which Are Natural Ceremonial Worship

Kneeling, bowing the body, prostration, lifting up the hands or the eyes toward heaven in the worship of God—these actions may in one sense be considered acts of worship themselves, and in another sense merely *circumstances* accompanying worship. They are acts of external worship when viewed as natural expressions of inward reverence. At the same time, they may be understood as circumstances of worship, being supportive additions to the more essential and substantial acts, to which they are sometimes necessarily joined. Yet the substantial parts of worship remain whole and complete even when these outward gestures are omitted.

Such gestures are naturally commendable, though not naturally *required*. Therefore, they ought to be used when they can be done conveniently and appropriately, and set aside when they cannot.

Some have referred to these and similar outward actions as *natural ceremonies*. They are called *natural* because nature itself teaches men to use them, apart from any divine or human institution (1 Corinthians 11:14: "Doth not even nature itself teach you..."). A rational man, by the light of nature alone, is guided to employ such expressions. Yet in these matters, natural guidance does not function without discretion and wise judgment. For the practice of such actions is shaped in part by the customs of various ages and countries, and by the particular circumstances of each case.

For example, standing in the acts of solemn declarations and engagements made to God—such as professing belief in the articles of the Christian faith, or affirming our consent to the covenant of grace—as well as in the offering of solemn praise and thanksgiving, such as the recitation of hymns of praise, is a natural expression of inward devotion. It is, therefore, an outward act of worship that is well-suited to the order of nature (Psalm 134:1: "Behold, bless ye the Lord, all ye servants of the Lord, which by night stand in the house of the Lord,").

§11. Concerning External Acts Which, by the Custom of the Age or Country, Express Devotion in Worship

It is often said that custom is a *second* nature. Some external actions, though grounded in custom, may be just as expressive and meaningful—at least in the eyes of men—as those derived directly from nature. The neglect of such customary expressions can appear unfitting or even offensive.

An example of this is the uncovering of the head by men during worship—such as removing their hat. In the worship of God, this act is a part of worship, for it is performed directly for His honor and expresses reverence of heart toward Him (1 Corinthians 11:4, "Every man praying or prophesying, having his head covered, dishonoureth his head,").

Yet I acknowledge that not every reverent gesture made in relation to God's worship is itself an act of worship. Some are merely accompanying features or adjuncts of worship, as will be explained later.

No ceremonial action—whether it be natural or customary—is required when natural weakness, illness, or some other necessity makes it unsuitable or unfit to be performed (Matthew 12:7: "But if ye had known what this meaneth, I will have mercy, and not sacrifice, ye would not have condemned the guiltless,").

§12. Concerning External Acts Which, by Divine Institution or General Custom of Nations, Express Divine Honor

The building of altars, the offering of sacrifices, and the burning of incense have, by the general practice of mankind, been regarded as acts of divine honor. Under the Law, these were explicitly set apart by God as forms of acknowledgment that belong to Him alone (Leviticus 1:9, "But his inwards and his legs shall he wash in water: and the priest shall burn all on the altar, to be a burnt sacrifice, an offering made by fire, of a sweet savour unto the Lord,"). Therefore, these actions are properly considered divine worship, regardless of the object to which they are directed. Indeed, even if the person offering them does not intend to acknowledge the object as a deity, these acts still constitute external divine worship—because they involve giving a form of honor that has been uniquely reserved for God.

The dedication of temples and the consecration of places to any being may admit of more than one interpretation. First, it may signify that the place is being set apart as sacred to that being, as the site of its worship, its special presence, and its influence among mortals. In that case, such a dedication is an act of divine worship. This, I believe, is the intent behind the Antichristian Roman Catholic practice of dedicating churches, chapels, and other places to saints and angels.

Second, such a dedication may mean nothing more than commemorating a created person—whether a saint or an angel—while still rendering all honor and service in the place solely to God. In this latter sense, to dedicate a church or other location to a created being is not to give divine honor to that being.

Similarly, the setting apart of days and times in honor of any person—if intended for invocation or for acts of service that belong to God—is an act of divine worship directed toward that person. But if days and times are set apart merely to commemorate a blessed person, and all honor and service on that day is directed to God alone, then this is not divine worship of that person.

§13. Concerning Fasting, Wearing of Sackcloth or Mean Apparel, Lying in Ashes, Going Barefoot, and Other Austerities Used in God's Worship

These actions are clear expressions of humility and self-abasement. Some of them—such as fasting and the wearing of plain or modest clothing—are fitting expressions of this in all ages and places (Joel 2:12, "Therefore also now, saith the Lord, turn ye even to me with all your heart, and with fasting, and with weeping, and with mourning,"). Others, such as lying in ashes or going barefoot, are only fitting in certain ages and cultures. Although these acts are naturally suited to convey humility, the particular expressions vary according to the customs of different times and places.

These practices are also appropriate means of mortification—some of them in all contexts (such as fasting), and others only in certain contexts, as dictated by cultural custom (Matthew 6:17-18, "But thou, when thou fastest, anoint thine head, and wash thy face; That thou appear not unto men to fast, but unto thy Father which is in secret...").

Therefore, such acts may be suitable adjuncts to divine worship on special occasions that call for solemn humiliation before God.

Moreover, these actions can themselves become acts of divine worship (whether they are rightly so used is another matter), when they are performed as direct means of honoring and pleasing God through the abasement and displeasure of self. In such a case, they are done before His footstool to magnify His name in our low and miserable condition (Isaiah 66:2, "To this man will I look, even to him that is poor and of a contrite spirit, and trembleth at my word,").

Indeed, Scripture explicitly warns of a kind of self-imposed worship that involves voluntary abasement and bodily neglect, which the Apostle terms "will-worship" (Colossians 2:23, "Which things have indeed a shew of wisdom in will worship, and humility, and neglecting of the body; not in any honour to the satisfying of the flesh,").

§14. Concerning the Nature of Monastic Vows of Obedience, Poverty, and Chastity

That the formal nature of these vows—as with all other vows—is an act of divine worship is not disputed. The question, rather, concerns the subject matter of these vows.

By the matter of these vows, their proponents intend a particular religious state that goes beyond the general religious state of Christianity itself. This special state is said to involve an obligation to certain duties and practices meant for the direct and immediate honor and service of God, and to carry this out in a higher and more perfected way than is found in the general calling of Christianity. Therefore, the substance of these vows is treated as a direct expression of devotion, or divine worship.

However, the matter of these vows may be purposed and handled in such a way that it becomes religious only in a secondary or indirect sense—that is, as a means of advancing religion. For example, it may be pursued to allow greater opportunity for spiritual exercises or greater liberty in spiritual warfare. On this basis, the celibate or single life was commended by the Apostle Paul—not that he commended the vow of celibacy, but the ongoing commitment to it for those purposes, provided the person had the gift or strength to remain in it (1 Corinthians 7:7–8: "For I would that all men were even as I myself... I say therefore to the unmarried and widows, It is good for them if they abide even as I,").

Whether such things are fitting subjects for vows, in this latter sense, is a matter to be considered further. The same reasoning may be applied to abstinence, as to celibacy.

§15. Concerning Decency and Order as Adjuncts of Divine Worship

The Apostle's rule—"Let all things be done decently and in order," (1 Corinthians 14:40),—is part of the law of nature and would bind the churches of Christ even if it had never been written in Scripture.

Decency, considered in itself, is not a part of worship but an adjunct to it. It is the proper outward arrangement or mode that corresponds with the dignity of the act. It is not unique to divine worship, but belongs equally to all serious civil and human actions. That is, any weighty or solemn matter should be conducted with suitable dress, posture, furnishings, and other signs of respect appropriate to a sacred occasion.

Order, likewise, is an *adjunct* of worship. It is not to be taken as a warrant for inventing new forms of worship, but only as a principle *for rightly arranging what already exists*. It involves the proper setting and structuring of the several parts of worship—such as method, measure, time, place, and other circumstances. It pertains to divine worship, not for any unique reason, but in the same way it applies to all human actions, where order brings both beauty and usefulness, and disorder brings confusion and harm.

The Apostle's rule concerns the kind of necessary decency and order, the absence of which results in indecency and disorder—not the use of elaborate attire, theatrical embellishments, pompous rituals, imagery, and various ornaments that appeal to the carnal mind. The decency that is commanded is that which suits things of a holy and reverent nature (Hebrews 12:28, "Wherefore we receiving a kingdom which cannot be moved, let us have grace, whereby we may serve God acceptably with reverence and godly fear,").

We can discern what is commanded in a law by considering what is forbidden in it. In this case, nothing is forbidden except indecency and disorder. Therefore, the only thing that is positively required is the kind of decency and order that directly opposes these faults. Plain reason confirms this: whatever is not indecent is decent, and whatever is not disorderly is orderly—assuming the subject is capable of bearing such attributes.

Most matters of decency and order are absolutely necessary only in a general sense. That is, there must be *some* form under the category, but not necessarily one specific form. The exact form to be used should be determined by sound judgment.

Some particular kinds of decency are intrinsically necessary when they are possible, because their opposites are inherently indecent. Others are necessary due to external circumstances, such as the customs of a particular time and place, or the quality and condition of persons involved. The first kind may be called *natural*, the second *civil* or *customary*. The latter are also necessary by the law of nature, though not directly, but indirectly—based on the assumption of those cultural circumstances. This second type, therefore, allows for much variation and change.

Choosing what is *less decent* over what is *more decent* takes on the nature of indecency, just as choosing a *lesser good* over a *greater good* may be counted as an evil choice. Still, in matters of this kind, it is neither wise nor safe to engage in excessive disputes over degrees—*more* or *less*—especially when such matters become controversial, scrupulous, or provoke suspicion. It is best to choose that which is most widely acceptable, provided there is no actual indecency involved. In such cases, no necessary decency has been neglected.

§16. Concerning Time and Place Considered as Adjuncts or as Matter of Worship

Time and place, in general, are necessary adjuncts or circumstances of divine worship. No natural or moral action can be carried out apart from them. These remain mere adjuncts when they attend upon divine worship in a manner and for a purpose common to all serious human actions—namely, when they are appointed and employed for convenience and for the suitable performance of the worship. In this sense, they serve the worship that is performed in them, but the worship itself does not arise from them.

However, time and place in God's worship can, at times, occupy a higher status and become part of the matter of worship itself—as in the case of the old Sabbath, the Lord's Day, the Tabernacle, and the Temple under the Mosaic dispensation. For when God, by His institution, appointed these times and places to be not merely incidental but permanently holy, making them a means of sanctifying His people, then the people, in submitting to that appointment—and in dedicating, observing, and sanctifying those times and places—performed specific acts of worship. Their observance was an oblation to God, a direct giving of honor to Him (Isaiah 58:13, "If thou turn away thy foot from the sabbath, from doing thy pleasure on my holy day... and shalt honour him...").

In such cases, these times and places were not only sanctified by the duties performed within them, but the duties themselves were, in part, sanctified and made acceptable by the holiness of the times and places.

Yet even in this elevated condition—when time and place are raised to be matters of worship—they still serve as adjuncts to that worship to which they belong and to which they are appropriated. This is because there exists, among the various parts of worship, a kind of hierarchy, where some elements may rightly be regarded as subordinate to others.

As God, by His own institution, can take times and places that are otherwise only adjuncts and raise them to be actual elements of worship—and has done so in the examples already named—so likewise, men may also, by their own institution, appoint times and places to be permanently holy and to be matters of worship, that is, to make an offering of them to God. Whether it is lawful for men to do so will be considered later. Nevertheless, whether instituted by God or by man, the act of dedicating and observing such times and places takes on the nature of worship. For the cause that institutes the act—whether divine or human—is something external to the formal nature of worship itself. The true essence of worship lies in the proper reason and direct aim of the action, regardless of who institutes it.

This leads to a question: does every adjunct of worship that is instituted by God, thereby become a matter or part of worship, which otherwise it would not be?

Some have claimed that under the Old Law, even the smallest ceremony prescribed by God was to be regarded as a part of worship. I do not presently evaluate that assertion to affirm or deny it. However, if it were so,

I would not attribute it solely to the fact that it was prescribed by God, but to some further reason. For I do not believe that God cannot prescribe a mere adjunct to worship without thereby changing its formal nature and making it into a distinct matter or element of worship. Rather, I hold that it may remain in its proper state as a *mere* adjunct.

Nevertheless, the act of observing an adjunct prescribed by God may itself be counted an act of worship—as every act of obedience to God may be so considered (Deuteronomy 11:1, "Therefore thou shalt love the Lord thy God, and keep his charge, and his statutes, and his judgments, and his commandments, always,"). Yet, in this discussion, we are speaking of worship not in the broad sense, but in the stricter sense.

§17. Concerning Sacred Signs and Significant Ceremonies in Divine Worship

A *sign* is something more apparent or familiar, used to reveal something less known or more hidden; or at the very least, it serves to further clarify or confirm the truth of something equally evident (Ezekiel 24:24, "Thus Ezekiel is unto you a sign: according to all that he hath done shall ye do...").

There are various types of signs: natural, customary, instituted, arbitrary, fixed, and occasional.

Just as things signified may be sacred or common, so may the signs themselves. And as with other things, there may be signs specific to worship.

Any sign that directly expresses worship is itself worship. All external worship is a sign of internal worship—whether it is sincere or false (Isaiah 29:13, "Wherefore the Lord said, Forasmuch as this people draw near me with their mouth... but have removed their heart far from me,"). Ceremonies which signify or express an act of worship are thus to be understood as ceremonial worship.

However, not all significant ceremonies are acts of worship, because not all of them signify or express worship.

Among the significant ceremonies that are true parts of worship, I include the sign of the cross in baptism, which is acknowledged as a sign of our dedication to Christ (Romans 6:3–4: "Know ye not, that so many of us as were baptized into Jesus Christ were baptized into his death?... we also should walk in newness of life,").

§18. Concerning the Nature of Holiness and the Distinctions of Holiness

Holiness in creatures refers either to a moral quality in angels and men—known as the image of God (Ephesians 4:24, "And that ye put on the new man, which after God is created in righteousness and true holiness,")—or to the relationship something bears to God, having been set apart or consecrated to Him.

In the most general sense, everything in heaven and earth belongs to the Lord (Psalm 24:1, "The earth is the Lord's, and the fulness thereof; the world, and they that dwell therein,"). But whatever is His in a special sense—set apart for His particular use—is called *holy*. This includes, first, *persons*: either those generally devoted to Him from the heart, such as all true believers and their children (1 Corinthians 7:14, "For the unbelieving husband is sanctified by the wife... else were your children unclean; but now are they holy,"); or those professing faith outwardly, such as all visible Christians; or, more specifically, those separated by office, such as the priests under the Old Covenant, and ministers of the Gospel now.

Second, *things* may be made holy—some by God's immediate command, others through general instructions given to man. Among these, some are more distantly, others more closely, set apart for Him. Things more closely or strictly consecrated to God include temples, utensils, land, and the like, which are holy by lawful separation and rightful dedication. Ministers are more holy than these material things, due to the closer relationship they bear to God. Things more remotely devoted to God include food, drink, homes, land, labor, and callings—everything that a godly man offers to God along with himself (1 Corinthians 10:31, "Whether therefore ye eat, or drink, or whatsoever ye do, do all to the glory of God,").

Indeed, as God sanctifies everything to the believer (1 Timothy 4:4–5: "For every creature of God is good… For it is sanctified by the word of God and prayer,"), so also the believer sanctifies everything to God. However, when we speak of holy things, we ordinarily refer not to those remote and general dedications, but to those more immediate and strictly defined for sacred use.

Some hold that true holiness consists in such a state of separation to holy purposes that the item can no longer be used for common purposes. But others consider this definition too narrow. For there may be temporary as well as permanent separation to sacred purposes, especially where those purposes more immediately relate to the worship and service of God. Not everything ultimately used for God's honor is to be called *holy* in this strict sense. As stated before, in a broader sense, all things used to the glory of God may be called holy.

Some argue that things which merely *accompany* worship in the same way they accompany other activities—such as time, place, furnishings, and so forth—are not sacred. They say that such things, though used in religious acts, remain civil in nature and do not change in substance or form, but only in relation to the subject they attend. To this I respond: when considered physically, things are neither civil nor sacred. They become one or the other based on how they are related and applied. Thus, many things of the same kind, when viewed merely in their natural form, may be civil at one time and sacred at another, depending on their use and relation. For example, the same physical action—such as bowing the body—may be an expression of civil respect in one setting, or of religious reverence in another (Psalm 95:6: "O come, let us worship and bow down: let us kneel before the Lord our maker,").

These things may accompany religion in a way that is physically common to other actions, but not morally or relationally so.

Some might say that these things serve the same function outside of divine worship as they do within it—for instance, using one's eyes to read any book. But this is only true in a physical sense, not in a moral or relational one. The *use* is the same physically, but not in relation or in meaning.

To explain this more clearly: religion presupposes civil order. Thus, holy things and actions necessarily require civil things and actions to accompany them as lower supports. Divine worship must be attended by many civil elements, which do not become sacred merely by their proximity to the sacred. For example, the clothing of ministers and congregants, the seating arrangement according to rank, and other civil formalities observed in religious assemblies remain civil in nature. They are not applied to religion as its adjuncts in a moral or spiritual sense, nor referred to a sacred use or purpose—except in the ultimate and general way that all things aim at the glory of God (1 Corinthians 10:31). They simply accompany religion in their subordinate, civil role.

Nevertheless, many things that are purely civil in everyday life become sacred in worship when their relative status is altered—when they are intentionally directed toward a religious purpose. For instance, bowing the body, lifting up the hands or eyes, or standing up, though physically the same, become sacred actions when employed in divine worship, and civil actions when used for civil ends.

Everything ought to be reverenced according to the *degree* and *measure* of its *holiness*.

The Second Part: Idolatry

§1. Concerning Superstition in General

Just as there can be a defect or deficiency in religion, so there can be an excess—and this excess is called superstition.

This excess does not consist in the formal principle of religion itself, for we cannot go too far in truly observing, reverencing, or loving God (Mark 12:30: "And thou shalt love the Lord thy God with all thy heart, and with all thy soul, and with all thy mind, and with all thy strength..."). Rather, the excess lies in the *undueness* either of the object or of the acts of religion, whether inward or outward.

When the excess concerns the object of religious worship—that is, when something unworthy or *unsuitable* is made the object of devotion—this is idolatry (Exodus 20:3: "Thou shalt have no other gods before me"). When the excess lies in the inward acts of religion, it appears in anxious scrupulosity, an overbearing sense of guilt, or other erratic and disproportionate thoughts about religious duty.

As for the external acts of religion, excess may arise either in *kind* or in *measure*. Excess in *kind* occurs when the act is something God has forbidden—whether specifically or under a general prohibition

(Deuteronomy 12:32: "What thing soever I command you, observe to do it: thou shalt not add thereto, nor diminish from it"). Excess in *measure* arises even in otherwise lawful acts, when such acts are pursued to such an extent that they cause the neglect of other required duties (Matthew 23:23: "...these ought ye to have done, and not to leave the other undone").

This kind of excess is more commonly found in *instituted* or *positive* worship than in *natural* worship, for natural worship is less prone to distortion when rightly understood.

To be *too religious*—that is, to add human inventions or extremes to divine worship—is, in a certain respect, to be *irreligious*. It can even amount to sacrilege when it deprives God of what is due in other areas of service. In every case, superstition lacks the essential character of *true religion*.

Superstition may be *positive*, involving acts of worship that are explicitly forbidden; or *negative*, consisting in religious abstinence from things that God has not forbidden. Some distinguish these two types accordingly. Yet I judge that, in the latter case, the essence of superstition does not lie simply in a *negation*— a mere abstaining—but rather in the particular religious *observance* concerning abstinence, and the conscience-bound *refusal* (Romans 14:14: "I know, and am persuaded by the Lord Jesus, that there is nothing unclean of itself:

but to him that esteemeth any thing to be unclean, to him it is unclean").

§2. Concerning Idolatry in General

Idolatry is a particular form of superstition, marked by excess in the object of worship. It consists in giving to that which is not God the kind of worship that belongs only to God (Isaiah 42:8: "I am the Lord: that is my name: and my glory will I not give to another, neither my praise to graven images").

An *idol*, in its most literal sense, is an image—a likeness or representation of some being. Most especially, it refers to something made to resemble either the true God or a false god. More broadly, an idol signifies anything—whether visible or invisible, real or imagined—that is worshipped as if it were God (Romans 1:23: "And changed the glory of the uncorruptible God into an image made like to corruptible man...").

An idol is not merely something that is avowed to be a god in place of the true God, but also anything to which any form of *divine honor* is given. Such honor, even in part, makes that object *functionally* another god.

If any incommunicable attribute of God—such as omniscience or the ability to search the heart—is ascribed to another, that other is made into another god, not in essence, but *so far as* such honor is given (Jeremiah 17:10: "I the Lord search the heart, I try the reins...").

Idolatry can be committed even by those who confess only the one true and living God. For though they may not profess more than one God, they can still give the divine honor of the one true God to something that they themselves do not even regard as divine (Ezekiel 14:3: "These men have set up their idols in their heart...").

To pray to any creature for benefits that only God can bestow—such as sending rain or fair weather—is to render divine worship to that creature and is, therefore, idolatry (Jeremiah 14:22: "Are there any among the vanities of the Gentiles that can cause rain? or can the heavens give showers? art not thou he, O Lord our God?").

§3. Concerning *Latria* and *Dulia*

As for the well-known distinction between *latria* and *dulia*, we will first examine the terms themselves, and then the meaning attributed to them by those who employ the distinction.

With regard to the words: *latria* is not used exclusively for worship given to God (Deuteronomy 28:48; Leviticus 23:7); nor is *dulia* used solely for worship rendered to creatures (Acts 20:19; Romans 12:11; 1 Thessalonians 1:9). *Latria* generally signifies all kinds of service, while *dulia* denotes a stricter kind of service—that of one who is not his own master but is completely subject to the will of another.

As for the meaning given by those who use this distinction: *latria* is defined as the worship in which the object is acknowledged to be the first cause and final end of all things; *dulia* as worship in which the object is not regarded in that way.

Yet this method of distinction does not create two kinds of worship in terms of the outward acts—these acts are the same in both *latria* and *dulia*, even among Romanists, with the exception of sacrifice. Nor does the distinction lie in the internal acts of the will—such as love, fear, and trust—which may be the same in both, and, through superstition, may be even greater in *dulia* than in *latria*. The distinction, then, exists only in an intellectual notion, which common people are unlikely to perceive.

Furthermore, even if the object is not conceived as the first cause and last end, it may still receive the kind of worship that belongs only to God—such as prayer, oaths, incense, dedication of temples and altars, and the making of vows (Matthew 4:10: "Thou shalt worship the Lord thy God, and him only shalt thou serve,").

The worship that Cornelius intended to give to Peter (Acts 10:25–26), and that John attempted to give to the angel (Revelation 22:8–9), exceeded what is due to creatures. Yet neither Cornelius nor John believed their respective objects to be the first cause or final end. Likewise, when the devil tempted Christ to fall down and worship him (Luke 4:7–8), he did not ask to be acknowledged as God, but Christ rebuked him for seeking the worship that belongs to God alone.

§4. Concerning Idolatry, Serious and Dissembled

Serious idolatry occurs when the mind consciously gives to a being that is not God the honor that belongs to God—or any part of it. It also occurs when one uses external signs of divine honor with the deliberate intent to give that honor to such a being.

In all serious or undissembled idolatry, there is some error—either about the *object* of worship or the *act* of worship. First, error about the object: either the thing worshipped is mistakenly believed to be God, or it is believed to possess some divine attribute or prerogative which it does not have. In these last two cases, the thing is worshipped not simply as God, but *as if* it were God in those respects.

Second, error about the act of worship: (1) when worship given to that which is not God is not recognized by the worshipper as divine worship, though it truly is; or (2) when worship understood to be divine is not perceived to be applied to the object, though in fact it is.

Dissembled idolatry is purely external. It consists in performing some outward sign of divine honor toward that which is not God, without intending in one's heart to honor it.

Yet every outward act commonly used to express divine worship is not, in itself, necessarily such an expression—when considered merely as a physical act. Therefore, not every such gesture constitutes idolatry in itself. But whenever such an act is knowingly and willingly performed at a time, in a place, and under circumstances that render it a recognized sign of divine worship, then the act is rightly interpreted as such. In that case, it is attributed to the person as if he had intended it as worship.

Although true worship includes internal reverence, and a mere sign without internal intention is not true worship, nevertheless, a man may give the outward appearance of that honor—even if it is false. In this way, he is truly guilty of idolatry, though of a dissembled kind. He gives the sign of divine honor to another, making outward show of bestowing upon another that which is owed to God alone (Isaiah 42:17: "They shall be turned back, they shall be greatly ashamed, that trust in graven images, that say to the molten images, Ye are our gods,").

Such a person, by outward profession, acknowledges another as the object of divine worship, thereby recognizing, in practice, another god. Though it may not be inward or mental, it is *bodily* idolatry. Just as an atheist may outwardly perform acts of worship to God while internally scorning Him, so also, a dissembler may outwardly perform acts of false worship, thereby becoming truly guilty of idolatry in a corporeal sense.

§5. Concerning Adoration Given to the Host

That Roman Catholics render divine worship to the Host is acknowledged by themselves, and it constitutes no small portion of their religion. *The Council of Trent* explicitly affirms that the same divine worship which is given to God Himself is to be given to the Most Holy Sacrament. By this, they mean the Body of Christ, believed to be present under the external appearances (*accidents*) of the bread.

According to Protestant doctrine, this amounts to the rendering of divine honor to a piece of bread, and is therefore a most senseless and monstrous form of idolatry (Isaiah 44:19: "And none considereth in his heart... shall I fall down to the stock of a tree?").

Some within the Protestant profession have attempted to lessen the severity of this by saying it is *material*, but not *formal* idolatry on the part of the Papists. Their reasoning is that the consecrated bread is believed to be the actual Christ, who is truly God. Therefore, even though the thing worshipped is not God in truth, it is believed to be God by those who worship it and is thus worshipped as such.

However, even some Roman Catholic writers have admitted that, if the doctrine of transubstantiation is an error, then the adoration of the Host amounts to the most vile and abominable idolatry. In that case, they cannot rely upon the material-formal distinction to excuse the act.

Furthermore, some Romanists have acknowledged that the words of institution—"This is my body" (Matthew 26:26)—may bear a figurative sense, as when Scripture says that Christ was a rock (1 Corinthians 10:4: "...and that Rock was Christ"). They have conceded that if Scripture alone were the only basis for transubstantiation, it would *not* suffice to establish it as an article of faith.

Bellarmine admits that these words must be understood either to indicate a real change in the bread, as the Roman Catholics claim, or a figurative sense, as the Calvinists maintain; but he rejects entirely the Lutheran position of consubstantiation. He concludes that while the words may contain ambiguity, that ambiguity is removed by the teaching of councils and church fathers.

The ancient Persians, during their idolatrous era, worshipped the sun as the supreme deity. Their error concerning the object of worship did not make their idolatry any less abominable (Deuteronomy 4:19: "And lest thou lift up thine eyes unto heaven, and when thou seest the sun, and the moon, and the stars... shouldest be driven to worship them..."). It was a case of *formal* idolatry, possessing the very essence and nature of that sin.

Indeed, it is a greater sacrilege and blasphemy against the true God to take any creature and imagine it to be Him—and then to worship it accordingly—than to give divine honor to a creature mistakenly thought to be a lower deity. For to take a created thing and ascribe to it the identity of the Most High is a deeper profanation.

Augustine, in his preface to his sermon on Psalm 93, refers to certain heretics who honored the sun, claiming it to be Jesus Christ. To give divine worship to the sun under that error is horrid idolatry. And why, then, should the giving of divine worship to a morsel of bread under the same delusion be any less so?

The Lutheran doctrine of consubstantiation does not lead to the adoration of the Eucharist. While they believe that Christ is truly present in the sacrament, they do not hold that the sacrament itself is Jesus Christ, nor do they worship it as such.

That said, to avoid exaggerating the error of the Papists regarding this *absurd* superstition of bread-worship, it should be noted that they do not take the bread to be the divine essence, nor the Deity itself—except insofar as it is identified with the human body of Christ, into which they believe the bread is changed. In this way, they claim to worship it as the Lord's body. Or, to put it in the most charitable terms, they worship Christ as being present there in His true body, and also worship the bread, supposing it to be that very body.

§6. Concerning the Popish Invocation of Angels and Departed Saints

This practice of *invocation* is entirely without precept or precedent in Holy Scripture. The Word of God directs us to call upon Him alone. Christ Himself, in His great rule and standard of prayer, teaches us to pray, "Our Father..." (Matthew 6:9). We are taught to invoke Him in whom we believe—namely, God alone (Romans 10:14: "How then shall they call on him in whom they have not believed?"). Just as incense, being the type, was to be offered to God alone, so also prayer—the reality signified—is to be offered to God alone (Revelation 8:4: "And the smoke of the incense, which came with the prayers of the saints, ascended up before God...").

Prayer is an act of that worship which the Romanists themselves call *latria*. It presupposes that the one addressed is the source and fountain of the good requested. Therefore, whoever is prayed to is treated as *standing in the place of God*. And though some claim that the saints are not invoked as authors of divine blessings, it is plainly evident that Roman Catholics pray to them directly and explicitly for such benefits—asking for health, deliverance, and even for the highest blessings, such as requesting St. Peter to open the gates of heaven. Their prayers are directed to the saints as though those saints have power at their own discretion to distribute the grace of God.

Moreover, prayer involves a full prostration of the soul, spirit, and body to the one invoked. It includes acts of submission, devotion, dependence, reverence, and the highest degree of veneration. Experience demonstrates the foolish passions that arise in these superstitious affections, where people are so taken with the objects of their devotion that they show them no less reverence than they offer to God and Christ. Indeed, they are so absorbed and overtaken with this misplaced love that they forget God altogether (Isaiah 42:8: "I am the Lord: that is my name: and my glory will I not give to another…").

If the saints are invoked as mediators, then they are treated as standing in the place of Christ. Yet Christ alone is our intercessor in heaven, and He is such because He is our Redeemer (1 John 2:1: "And if any man sin, we have an advocate with the Father, Jesus Christ the righteous,"). Therefore, those who are not our redeemers *cannot* be intercessors for us in heaven.

Additionally, we cannot reasonably commend our prayers to any being unless we are assured both that they can hear us and that they will present our requests before God.

The Roman Catholic invocation of saints and angels attributes to them the incommunicable excellencies of God—such as being able to search hearts, to know the conditions and concerns of all who pray to them, and to possess a kind of omniscience and omnipresence—if not absolute, yet at least with respect to all things under heaven.

In an attempt to excuse this sacrilege and idolatry, they have devised the incredible notion that the saints behold all things *in speculo Trinitatis*—in the mirror of the Trinity. But this is a vain and presumptuous invention. Even the human nature of Christ, though hypostatically united to the divine nature, never laid claim to such omniscience on its own (Mark 13:32: "But of that day and that hour knoweth no man, no, not the angels which are in heaven, neither the Son, but the Father,"). To fabricate such a fiction is an arrogant encroachment upon God's prerogative.

In truth, the worship of saints and angels maintained in the Roman Church closely parallels the worship of *demons* among the pagans. These *demons* were believed to be either the souls of departed men or other invisible powers, imagined to be lesser deities subordinate to and serving the supreme god. In similar fashion, the Roman Church has appointed among the saints various patron protectors of provinces, cities, trades, living creatures, and more—just as the heathens once did.

When we ask holy persons on earth to pray for us, we do not approach them as patrons or mediators on the basis of their merits. Rather, we ask them as brethren, standing before God on the same level with us. Such mutual help is in keeping with the communion of saints, and it is supported by divine promise, command, and example (James 5:16: "Pray one for another... The effectual fervent prayer of a righteous man availeth much,").

§7. Concerning the Erecting of Altars and the Bringing of Oblations to Any Besides God

Those outward actions which, by nature, by long-standing custom, or by divine institution, are or have been exclusively used to express the inward reverence and honor due to God alone, are acts of divine worship. Among such actions are the erecting of altars, the offering of oblations, the burning of incense, the making of vows, the dedication of temples, and the appointment of religious festivals (Exodus 30:1-3; Psalm 66:13-14).

To erect an altar—whether for the purpose of sacrifice or for any other kind of offering—to any being, implies either a belief that this being acts as an avenger of sin in a manner beyond human judgment and punishment, and that it may be propitiated; or it implies a grateful acknowledgment of benefits believed to come from a higher source than any earthly benefactor—that is, from a sovereign providence. But whatever being is thus propitiated or acknowledged must be either the Most High God, or a supposed lesser deity to whom is ascribed what God has never given or shared with any creature.

Beyond the intrinsic reasoning of the matter, the universal practice of mankind and the express ordinances of God have established such actions as specific to divine worship. If it is considered a great presumption to render to a human subject the form of honor which a sovereign ruler has reserved exclusively to himself, how much more arrogant and sacrilegious is it to use those signs of divine honor—reserved by God for Himself alone—in the service of any creature (Isaiah 42:8: "I am the Lord: that is my name: and my glory will I not give to another...").

Even though, under the new covenant, God has done away with certain outward modes of worship—such as the use of altars, sacrifices, and offerings whether propitiatory or eucharistic—since the purpose of those forms has passed with the coming of Christ, yet to apply those same forms to any creature remains idolatrous. Although these forms are now set aside in Christian worship, they still retain the imprint and meaning of divine honor (Hebrews 10:12: "But this man, after he had offered one sacrifice for sins for ever, sat down on the right hand of God,").

Therefore, to erect altars or to bring offerings to any being besides the true and living God is an act of idolatry.

§8. Concerning Making Vows to Any Besides God

Both divine ordinance and the longstanding custom of mankind have established that making vows is a distinct act of divine worship (Deuteronomy 23:21: "When thou shalt vow a vow unto the Lord thy God, thou shalt not slack to pay it: for the Lord thy God will surely require it of thee; and it would be sin in thee,").

Therefore, to direct a vow to any creature is a form of idolatry.

According to sound reason, a vow is indeed an act of worship. To vow unto God is to express inward subjection and devotion to Him, as well as trust in Him as the sovereign ruler over our lives and all that concerns us (Psalm 76:11: "Vow, and pay unto the Lord your God: let all that be round about him bring presents unto him that ought to be feared,").

While earnest and solemn promises made to men on earth may metaphorically be termed vows, and things set aside for the use or service of individuals might be described as "devoted" to them, such uses of language are figurative. The Popish practice of making vows to departed saints, however, partakes of the same nature as vows made to God, for they involve inward subjection, spiritual devotion, and a kind of reliance that belongs only to divine worship.

At times, the very *content of vows* made to saints includes religious acts—such as praying to them, offering oblations, or dedicating temples to their name. At other times, the vow may involve promising to do something toward others on earth (*e.g.*, to give a certain amount to the poor), but even in these cases, the vow, in its essential form, represents a religious subjection and devotion to the saint, viewed as an invisible celestial power—anticipating blessing if the vow be kept, and divine retribution if it be broken.

It is no defense for these Papists to argue that they do not render such vows to saints as to sovereign first causes, but only in a subordinate respect. For the things which God alone claims—such as the full prostration of the soul, the submission of the conscience, and the dependence on supernatural governance—are ascribed to these departed creatures. Though they claim this to be in a lesser degree, they nonetheless offer to the saints that which is due only to the Lord (Isaiah 42:8).

This closely mirrors the ancient idolatry of the Gentiles, who erected altars, made vows, offered sacrifices, and prayed to the souls of dead men or to other demons—acknowledging them not as supreme gods but as lesser divine powers. If such worship of inferior spirits was not idolatry, then idolatry scarcely existed among the Romans. But indeed, this was one of its chief forms. The Roman Church has followed suit, treating the departed saints as inferior deities, even borrowing the titles *Divi* and *Divae* from the old pagan tongue.

Furthermore, to make a vow to a saint presumes the saint's ability to hear and receive such a vow. This, in turn, presumes an omniscience that includes the knowledge of all earthly matters, and even the hidden intents of the heart. Such a quality is divine (1 Kings 8:39: "Then hear thou in heaven thy dwelling place, and forgive... for thou, even thou only, knowest the hearts of all the children of men,"). Therefore, by such supposition, they ascribe to the saints a prerogative that belongs to God alone, and thereby commit idolatry.

§9. Concerning Burning Incense to Any Besides God

The burning of incense in the Old Testament is a form of worship that God has explicitly reserved for Himself alone (Exodus 30:7-9: "And Aaron shall burn thereon sweet incense every morning... Ye shall offer no strange incense thereon,"). Therefore, to offer incense to any angel, saint, or creature, is to commit idolatry.

This act represented spiritual service—prayer, praise, and thanksgiving—ascending acceptably to God, as a sweet savor (Psalm 141:2: "Let my prayer be set forth before thee as incense; and the lifting up of my hands as the evening sacrifice,"). Since incense signifies that spiritual communion which is proper to God, it cannot be lawfully offered to any creature.

Moreover, incense was burned in the holy place by the priest while the people prayed in the outer court, thereby typifying the intercession of Jesus Christ, our High Priest, before God (Luke 1:10-11). Being so, the rite is an emblem of divine mediation, and thus constitutes an act of divine worship. If this is transferred to any other, it is a plain act of idolatry.

§10. Concerning the Dedicating of Places and Times, and the Erecting of Symbolical Presence to Any Besides God

Such actions—dedicating sacred spaces or appointing times for worship—have always been reserved to God, and are to be used as acts of worship directed toward Him alone. In this way, to dedicate temples, chapels, groves, or any place as the particular seat or presence of a saint or angel—as the Papists do—is idolatry. It falsely directs worship to one who is not God.

However, to set apart places for the sole worship of God, and in remembrance of His servants, without rendering them worship, is not idolatrous. A building named after a saint may be tolerable, so long as it is truly devoted to God's worship alone, and no religious service is rendered to the creature (e.g., 2 Chronicles 6:10: Solomon built a house to "the name of the Lord God of Israel," not to David).

The same applies to the dedication of days and seasons. To appoint a day for honoring God by remembering His work in or through a servant may be lawful, if rightly ordered. But to sanctify a day to a saint as the object of worship is a *breach* of the first and second commandments.

Erecting a symbol of divine presence, such as the Ark or Mercy Seat, was ordained by God for His own worship. To mimic this for any creature—setting up a statue, image, or altar as a visible representation of a saint or angel's presence, and bowing before it—is to render them divine honor, and is therefore idolatry

(Exodus 20:5: "Thou shalt not bow down thyself to them, nor serve them,").

§11. Concerning the Worship of Relics

Relics may include not only bodily remains of Christ or the saints, but also things that belonged to them—such as clothing, personal items, or supposed fragments of the cross. The Roman Church asserts that relics of Christ are to be worshipped with the worship due to Christ Himself, and the relics of saints with the worship due to the saints. By this declaration, they convict themselves of manifest idolatry.

One may rightly show respect to the relics of loved ones, ancestors, or public benefactors—such as keeping a letter or garment of a parent. But this is mere civil reverence, not religious worship. It is vastly different from kneeling before bones and garments in religious acts, or attributing to them divine power.

To use relics to drive away evil spirits, or to obtain protection and favor, is not only superstition, but *blind* and *brutish* error. It aligns not with Scripture, but with the folly of heathenism. True safety is in Christ alone, not in fragments of matter preserved in gold boxes. (Jeremiah 10:5: "They are upright as the palm tree, but speak not: they must needs be borne, because they cannot go. Be not afraid of them; for they cannot do evil, neither also is it in them to do good,").

§12. Concerning the Worship of the Cross

To worship the cross (commonly called *staurolatry*) is idolatry.

It remains a question whether many Roman Catholics, in their veneration of the cross and of relics, intend more than a high regard or reverential honor. It may be that not all are so blind as to pray to these objects, or to look for aid from them as if they were principal causes of help, but rather regard them as instruments or secondary means.

However, even granting *that*, there is no legitimate ground for veneration or reverence toward the cross due to its association with Christ. The cross was the very tool employed by Christ's murderers in their cruelty. It was no more a cause of salvation than were the Roman soldiers who nailed Him to it. The cross did not accomplish salvation as an active agent. Rather, Christ accomplished salvation *on* the cross, not *by* it—when the term is taken in its literal, physical sense and not metaphorically (Colossians 2:14: "Blotting out the handwriting of ordinances that was against us... and took it out of the way, nailing it to his cross,").

When Paul speaks of glorying in the cross of Christ (Galatians 6:14: "But God forbid that I should glory, save in the cross of our Lord Jesus Christ,"), he speaks figuratively. He means Christ crucified, and the atonement accomplished thereby—not the wooden beams themselves.

Moreover, even if the cross were to be gloried in, it would not follow that it should be revered, much less worshipped. One may glory in enduring shame or suffering for Christ's sake, but that does not mean the instruments of that suffering are to be venerated. The apostle rejoiced to suffer for Christ, yet he did not bow to prison bars or scourges. Therefore, to render worship to the physical cross is baseless and idolatrous.

§13. Whether Christ as Man, or Mediator, is to be Worshipped

Let these principles be laid down:

1. There is but one immediate, formal, and adequate reason for Divine Worship—namely, the supreme majesty, independent and infinite excellency of the eternal Godhead.
2. All Divine Worship, by its nature, is the highest form of honour and observance that may be rendered, because its formal object and ground is the infinite and supreme excellence of the Divine being.
3. Though the Godhead is necessary for Christ's mediation, mediation itself is not necessary to the Godhead.
4. Our faith does not rest finally and absolutely, but mediately, upon Christ as our Mediator, who is both God and man (1 Timothy 2:5).

5. The mediatory power and glory of Christ as God-man is distinct from His natural and essential glory as eternal God (John 17:5).

Therefore, concerning the question: Christ the Mediator, who is God and man, is indeed to be worshipped—as the Scriptures clearly affirm (Revelation 1:6; Revelation 5:8, 12–14; Romans 14:9). Yet from the foregoing principles, it is proven that He is to be worshipped with divine worship not *as Mediator* per se, but as *God*. Christ *as Mediator* is the material or terminative object of worship—that is, the one worshipped—but not the *formal* object or ground of that worship. If, hypothetically, our Mediator were not God (though this is impossible), He could not lawfully receive divine worship (Isaiah 42:8: "I am the LORD: that is my name: and my glory will I not give to another,").

It is true that Christ is worshipped as Mediator if one takes "as Mediator" to describe the *person* being worshipped—but not as a *formal reason* for that worship. Therefore, all divine worship given to Christ affirms His *divine nature*.

Although the office of Christ is not the formal basis for adoration, it provides a powerful motive for rendering Him worship due to His infinite majesty and authority.

When one prays, "Lord Jesus, pray for me," the address is made to Him as God, though the action requested—intercession—is performed by Him as man,

(Romans 8:34: "It is Christ that died... who also maketh intercession for us,"). And this intercession is carried out in a way suitable to the coessential and eternal Son of God.

Christ is not adored *formally* as Judge, but He is adored because He *is* Judge—judging by divine authority. The divine nature is the principal agent in judgment (John 5:22), while the human nature acts by instrument and association.

In His mediatory work, Christ performs divine operations—not by the office formally, but as that office resides in a divine person. Some have added that such operations, proceeding from the Mediator, are *impulsive* causes (*i.e.*, they prompt adoration), but not *formal* reasons for adoration.

Wherever the divinity is communicated to the humanity of Christ, worship is also properly communicated—specifically by reason of the *hypostatic union* (Colossians 2:9: "For in him dwelleth all the fulness of the Godhead bodily,"). The divine nature, with all its infinite and adorable attributes, resides in the humanity of Christ, such that *the man Christ Jesus* is not worshipped *as man*, but as united personally to the eternal Son.

In this way, in our worship of Christ, the worship is directed to His person as the God-man, but the foundation and ground of the worship is drawn wholly from His eternal deity.

§14. Of Worshipping Images, or of Idolatry in the Mediate Object of Worship

An image is a likeness or representation of something, and its use in religious worship is to *signify* the one it represents.

Broadly speaking, the term "image" may include any object used to signify another, even if it does not physically resemble the thing represented—for example, the use of an uncut stone to signify Neptune.

A symbolic presence is not the same as an image. A symbol merely indicates the presence of something in a general or indirect way, while an image purports to present the thing itself. For this reason, God permitted symbols of His presence but strictly forbade making any image of Himself (Deuteronomy 4:15–16: "Take ye therefore good heed unto yourselves... lest ye corrupt yourselves, and make you a graven image, the similitude of any figure...").

The worship of an image can be considered in two ways: either as directed to the material of the image—wood, stone, metal, and so on—or to the being the image is intended to represent, usually a supposed deity.

Furthermore, a physical image may be regarded as more than a mere symbol. Some may consider it to be animated or even an embodiment of a deity, so that the worship is aimed both at the material and the invisible spiritual being, as though together they formed one body-soul compound.

Worship directed at a mere image is never due to its physical composition (*e.g.*, wood or stone), but only due to its resemblance to the thing it portrays. The image is worshipped not as the final object of devotion, but as a medium through which worship is directed to the ultimate object, the prototype. Thus, in such cases, the prototype is worshipped *in* the image.

Consequently, the worship offered to the image must be of the same kind as the worship due to the prototype. If it is not, then it terminates on the image itself and does not pass through it. In other words, if the worship differs in kind, then it is not mediate but absolute—and idolatrous.

Those who worship images are not agreed about the type of worship due to them. Bellarmine, for instance, argues that the worship properly given to the image as the terminating object is a sort of incomplete, analogical worship—neither *latria* (divine worship), *hyperdulia* (special veneration for Mary), nor *dulia* (honor to saints)—but something imperfect, pointing to these higher forms as its end.

But this means, that in order to avoid idolatry, the worshipper must understand and navigate intricate distinctions: *latria*, *dulia*, *hyperdulia*; direct versus indirect; proper versus improper; simple versus qualified; analogical and reductive categories. Is this the kind of theological acrobatics that should safeguard the soul from the anger of a jealous God (Exodus 20:5: "for I the LORD thy God am a jealous God..."), all for the sake of promoting a form of worship that God *never* commanded?

An inanimate thing has no excellence in itself that could merit religious honor. It cannot deserve reverence as an object of worship in its own right. Therefore, a mere material image cannot rationally or rightly be the final object of worship. But if the image is regarded as the body of a living being or a deity in bodily form, then it becomes the absolute object of the worship offered to it—which is plainly idolatrous.

Worship directed toward a symbolic presence is not worship of the symbol itself. For example, bowing before a king's throne is not worship of the throne, but of the sovereign who sits on it. Likewise, when Israelites turned toward the Mercy Seat in the Most Holy Place, they were not worshipping the Mercy Seat itself (Exodus 25:21–22). It was a means or direction of worship—not the object of it.

Scripture speaks often and forcefully about the idolatry of image-worship, because it is one of the most prevalent forms of idolatry, and is often interwoven with all others. Both true and false gods have historically been worshipped by idolaters, through the use of images (Isaiah 44:17–19; Psalm 115:4–8). This type of idolatry must be considered both in its use in the worship of false gods and also in its use in the corrupted worship of the true God.

§15. Of the Worshipping of False Gods in Images

Among the heathens, the images of their gods were called "gods"—not properly, but figuratively—just as a portrait of a man might be called "a man." No reasonable person could believe that a mere statue or painting is, in itself, a god. In this respect, the heathens were no more guilty than the Papists.

The heathens believed that their gods resided in the images, and that power was exercised through them. In the same way, the Papists treat their sacred images as special residences of God, Christ, the saints, and angels—and worship those images with the kind of reverence that belongs to God alone. In doing so, they turn these images into idols.

In former times, the devil—by God's permission—dwelt and worked through certain images, making them infamous and leading people to worship them with special fervor. Similarly, Papists believe that some images have divine or supernatural power attached to them more than others.

The common heathen people, being misled by satanic delusions, could be easily brought to worship the images themselves. These statues were decorated in ways that amazed and terrified onlookers, leading them to imagine that the image itself was divine—not as the full deity, but as the bodily form inhabited by an unseen god. In much the same way, many uneducated and superstitious Roman Catholics today may fall into the same gross error.

This may explain why the prophets worked so earnestly to show that idols and images are not gods (Isaiah 44:9-20; Jeremiah 10:3-5).

Just as the more informed Papists say they only view the images as representations of the beings to whom they offer divine worship, so too did the more educated heathens make that same claim.

And just as the wiser among the heathens disagreed with the common people about the nature of the gods, yet still participated with them in all external forms of worship, so do the educated Papists join the unlearned in all their outward acts of idolatry.

Therefore, to worship a false god by means of an image is to commit a double idolatry: first, by giving divine worship to something that is not God as the ultimate object; and second, by giving worship to the image as a mediate object in relation to the first.

§16. Of Making Images of the True God

An image intended to represent the true God is, by definition, an idol—such as the golden calf made in the wilderness or the calves set up in Dan and Bethel, (Exodus 32:4-5; 1 Kings 12:28-30).

To *attempt* to make an image of God is to blaspheme Him. God's infinite nature cannot be represented by any finite form without bringing dishonor to His majesty. It is an inherent degradation.

Some may ask, "May not God be represented by the visible forms in which He once appeared?" The answer is no. In the burning bush (Exodus 3:2–6), or in the glory on Mount Sinai (Exodus 24:16–17), God did not appear as an image of Himself, but rather through appointed signs or symbols of His presence. Whether it was God or merely angels who appeared to Abraham or Jacob in human form is debated—but even if it was God the Son in a pre-incarnate form, He did not assume those appearances as images or representations of the divine essence, but as signs that marked divine presence and purpose.

Man's soul is said to be the image of God, but only in a figurative, improper, and metaphorical sense (Genesis 1:26–27). Even so, that spiritual image cannot be captured by art, and an image of man's body is not even a true image of the image of God.

No image fashioned by human hands can capture the excellency by which God is distinct from all creation.

Indeed, the virtues of the human mind are more picturable than God Himself.

God strictly prohibited Israel from making any image of Him and gave this reason: that when He appeared at Mount Sinai, they saw no form or similitude, (Exodus 20:4; Deuteronomy 4:15–16).

It is foolish to argue that only images attempting a perfect likeness are forbidden, and that analogical or symbolic representations are permitted. No one—heathen or otherwise—believes a carved image could perfectly represent God. Even those pagans who acknowledged an eternal deity never thought their statues were perfect representations. So then, did God make a law prohibiting what is impossible, yet allow every false and limited representation that men could devise? That is absurd.

The cherubim were not images of God; they were hieroglyphical symbols ordained by God for the purpose of signifying His presence, not representing His nature, (Exodus 25:18–22).

To create an image of fire or rays of light to signify the unapproachable light in which God dwells (1 Timothy 6:16), or to inscribe His name among such depictions, is not to create an image of Him but rather to employ a form of symbolic or pictorial writing.

When Moses saw what Scripture refers to as God's "back parts," it was not God Himself, but a created glory (Exodus 33:23).

There is a vast difference between our limited intellectual conceptions of God in the mind and the presumptuous, unworthy representations of Him to the senses. All that we may conceive rightly is that God is a being of infinite perfection—this is a mental understanding, not a material image or sensory impression.

§17. Of Worshipping the True God in Images

To worship God by means of an image does not glorify Him as God, but rather *diminishes* His majesty through a false representation.

When one says they worship God in an image, they necessarily give divine honor to the image itself—though it be termed relative. In so doing, the image becomes a false god, an idol, and the worship due only to God is misapplied to a creature. Scripture thus calls the golden calf an idol (Exodus 32:4, 8; 1 Kings 12:28–30).

To worship God as though He animates an image is likewise idolatry.

To treat an image as *medium cultum*—that is, as the thing mediately worshipped, on the basis of it representing God while the worship is said to terminate in God Himself—is *exactly* what the Second Commandment forbids (Exodus 20:4–5). It is not *merely* the making of the image that is condemned, but the use of it in the service of divine worship, even if the worship is not terminated in the image.

It appears also that the Second Commandment forbids even the use of images as *medium cultus*—that is, as a medium in God's worship though not themselves worshipped. The commandment does not permit visual representations of God as mere helps to devotion, for God has forbidden the employment of such representations in His worship altogether.

It is not unlawful to create images of things other than God—such as depictions of holy men—so long as they are not worshipped, but merely serve as objects to stimulate consideration, reflection, or remembrance.

A question may be raised whether a crucifix or pictorial image of Christ in His human form may lawfully be used in this fashion. If it is permitted to own a depiction of Christ's human body, could that not serve as a help to devotion?

However, since the Second Commandment forbids the worship of God by means of *any* representation—even if that representation is not itself the object of worship—it must be doubted whether such a use of Christ's image in devotion is lawful. Though Christ is rightly worshipped in His person, that worship is grounded in His *divine nature*. Moreover, the danger is significant: that the image itself becomes the object of veneration.

For this reason, it is unsafe to use a crucifix or any fixed image of Christ according to His human form as a settled representation. It is the peril of idolatry which is far too near.

§18. Of Material Images and Representations Not of God, but of Other Things Used in God's Worship, and of the Symbols of the Divine Presence; of Worshipping Towards the East, and Bowing Towards the Altar

Divine Worship

To create images or representations for use in divine worship is not inherently sinful in every case. This is evident from examples such as the bronze serpent, which was ordained temporarily by God for a specific occasion in the wilderness (Numbers 21:8–9), and the cherubim atop the mercy seat, which were appointed as a standing ordinance under the Mosaic dispensation (Exodus 25:18–22).

There were also supernatural and unimitable manifestations, not of the divine essence, but of God's presence—such as the burning bush (Exodus 3:2–4) and the visible glory on Mount Sinai (Exodus 19:18–20). These were not images of God but symbols of His presence.

However, to direct divine worship to such images or representations as if they were *mediate* objects of that worship is idolatry. The ark, the cherubim, and the temple were never appointed as objects of worship. A learned writer has said that religious bowing toward any symbolical presence as though it were an object of devotion is *outright idolatry*. If done in honor of saints, angels, or demons, it is a twofold idolatry; if in honor of the true God, it remains idolatry nonetheless, though of a lesser sort.

There is a difference between using something (*e.g.*, the ark, the mercy seat, the temple) as an aid to our reflection and attention in worship, and making it an object of worship itself. That same author affirms that adoration directed toward a supernatural and unimitable manifestation of the divine presence is not idolatry—meaning that something like the burning bush or the fiery glory on the mountain served as a medium through which God's presence shone, and not as an object in itself to be worshipped.

Whether one may construct a symbolical presence of God by human invention is questionable. It seems to me to be an act of great presumption and arrogance. For it cannot be known with certainty—at least not by men—whether under the gospel administration God resides more in one place than another. And from our Savior's words, "The hour cometh, when ye shall neither in this mountain, nor yet at Jerusalem, worship the Father," (John 4:21), many have rightly concluded that no local confinement of God's presence is now to be expected.

God's special presence with His people—especially during worship—is real, but it is different in kind from His presence in any physical location. This presence He has promised *in His Word* (Matthew 18:20), and the reason for it is plain: it is not tied to a building, but to His people assembled in His name.

Therefore, for anyone to consider temples, or communion tables (often improperly called altars), as if they were a *Shechinah* or a divine habitation, is unjustified. Likewise, to call the communion table the throne of Christ (*Solium Christi*), as some have done, is unwarranted.

To lift the eyes and hands toward heaven in prayer or praise is both proper and scriptural, for God declares, "Heaven is my throne, and earth is my footstool," (Isaiah 66:1). He has revealed that He dwells in the heavens with the greatest manifestation of His visible glory (Psalm 115:3; Ecclesiastes 5:2).

The early churches that worshipped facing east did not worship the east as a mediate object, and thus were not guilty of idolatry. Their posture may have carried a symbolic meaning, perhaps alluding to Christ as the "Dayspring from on high" (Luke 1:78) or the "Sun of righteousness" (Malachi 4:2). Whether or not this practice was expedient is a separate matter and I leave it undecided.

I believe those in our time who bow toward the altar—so called—do not intend to worship the altar itself. Some explain the gesture as no different in kind than removing one's hat in church—an act of reverence toward God or toward the setting apart of the place for holy use. Such gestures, in themselves, do not make the building, the furniture, or any part of it the object of worship.

Others, however, may regard the altar as a symbol of Christ's throne or a representation of His presence, which is unlawful. To bow on that basis is a culpable act.

Still others may hold a merely mystical view of the gesture, as with the ancient practice of facing east. Some may do it purely for the sake of uniformity—

arguing that since bowing to God when entering or leaving church is proper, it is likewise fitting to bow in the same direction consistently.

The prudence or propriety of this practice, I leave unresolved.

§19. Of the Scandalous Use of Images

The presence of images, especially those to which others give unlawful worship, may be a cause of stumbling. In countries dominated by Roman Catholic practices, having images such as crucifixes, statues of the Virgin Mary, saints, or angels can provoke scandal and misunderstanding. For this reason, and due to the danger of idolatry, it is better not to possess them at all.

To place such images in churches constitutes a public stumbling-block, as it presents a temptation to some to worship them. At best, such images do more *harm* than good.

The historical use of images in worship—such as using them to remember biblical events or to stir devotion—is dangerous, especially when the images depict the object of worship, like a crucifix or picture of Christ. This tends to *pollute* the mind with idolatrous notions or hinders the proper spiritual engagement of the soul, which is the ordinary effect of such representations.

Images of false deities, or depictions of supposed divine powers that may tempt someone to believe in or worship them, are entirely unlawful.

Even the use of old symbols of divine presence—such as those from the Mosaic economy—set before the eyes during worship for the sake of remembrance or to stir affection toward God is perilous and to be avoided.

§20. Of the Mere Appearance of Idolatry in Any Kind

By "mere appearance of idolatry," I do not mean actual bodily acts of idolatry, which are outward signs of inward worship, even if the worship is only feigned. Rather, I refer to actions that merely seem to be such signs, even when they are not.

There is a question to be raised about bowing toward the altar or communion table: does this not create an appearance of idolatry, especially to the common people or to those less skilled in distinguishing between worship directed *to* an object and worship done merely *toward* it?

This concern is even greater when worship is directed toward a crucifix or other religious images, even if only meant as *aids* to remembrance.

Likewise, when expressions of reverence toward saints or angels are mixed into the worship of God, even if those expressions are not exclusive to divine worship but are shared with civil honor, such mixtures may still convey an appearance of idolatry. Even if one tries to distinguish between veneration and worship, for the sake of avoiding scandal, it may be wiser to forgo such expressions altogether.

The same risk of appearance occurs when bowing to a king or magistrate during the time of divine worship—unless the timing, custom, and manner of the act clearly distinguish it from religious adoration.

Furthermore, if a king were to adopt an action common to both civil and religious honor and assign it as a token of divine worship to himself—then for anyone to use that action toward him or his image, even with a civil intent, without protest against its idolatrous meaning, would carry the appearance of giving him divine honor.

§21. Whether a Course of Idolatry in What Kind Soever Infer a State of Damnation

The question concerns whether all forms of idolatry constitute mortal sin—not merely in terms of guilt or desert, but in actual effect—that is, whether the habitual practice of any kind of idolatry necessarily indicates the absence of saving grace and the indwelling of the sanctifying Spirit.

It is evident that not all idolatry, in every degree, is of this damning nature. Idolatry, in its broadest sense, is the giving of honor to the creature which is due to the Creator alone (Romans 1:25). This is not limited to formal and declared acts of worship, but includes the secret affections of the heart. Thus, there are "idols of the world" (*idola seculi*) as well as "idols of the temple" (*idola templi*). And it is sadly common among sincere worshippers of God to rob Him of honor and place it upon the creature—habitually so, though in a subdued and not prevailing measure. The lingering presence of covetousness, which is idolatry (Colossians 3:5), stands as proof of this.

If this may be true in reference to inward idols of the heart, why may it not also be so in the case of external idols of the temple? Indeed, it may be more excusable in the latter case—particularly in devout persons who live in spiritually darker times and places—because their misdirected worship may proceed not from loving the creature more than God, but from ignorance and error regarding the proper means of worship (Acts 17:30).

Therefore, there is no doubt that many holy souls in such benighted ages and countries have been habitually guilty of a lesser form of idolatry—making idols to themselves, not as being God simply, but as intermediaries or subordinates (*cf.* Exodus 32:4-5). The undue honour they rendered to the creature did not overturn the sincerity of their devotion to God, nor nullify their heartfelt and prevailing commitment to give the highest glory to Him alone.

Such people may truly and prevalently acknowledge the living God, along with all the essentials of true religion. As such, they may rightly be reckoned among the true Church of God—"true" being taken here for the essence and substance of the Church, not for its full integrity or spiritual health (1 Kings 19:18).

The Third Part: Superstition

§1. Of Excess in the Quantity or Measure of Religious Observances

All *superstition* is an *excess* in religion. The excess in the object of worship, already addressed in the Second Part, being set aside, it now remains to consider the excess that pertains to religious acts themselves. This kind of excess occurs either in the measure or in the kind, whenever the rule of religion is transgressed by going beyond what is appointed. In some instances, both kinds of excess may be present together.

Excess in the *quantity* or *measure* of religious observances occurs when the act, though lawful in kind, exceeds what is profitable or edifying in degree, and even becomes a hindrance to true religion. For example, prayer or preaching that is overly long or conducted at unseasonable times; an overly rigid insistence on religious exercises upon the Lord's Day or any other lawful time appointed, in such a way that it contradicts the works of mercy, or present necessity, or even that suitable liberty of life and mutual converse which does not distract the mind from God. Likewise, an over-anxious care for the minutiae of decency and order, and a needless accumulation of rites and ceremonies, may also be superstitious.

§2. Of Excess in Religious Observances, for the Kind Thereof

Excess in the *kind* of religious observance occurs when man, under the guise of honoring God, presumes to offer him such acts of worship as he has either expressly forbidden or has never commanded, and which are not pleasing to him.

God may forbid particular kinds of religious observances either by specific prohibitions, such as when he explicitly banned certain heathen practices from Israel; or by general rules which prohibit all acts of worship of a similar nature and rationale.

Some kinds of religious observance are intrinsically unlawful because they are morally corrupt and unsuitable for the Holy God—such as those forms of worship offered to *Bacchus* and other pagan deities, whose service corresponded to their impure character. These acts are vicious in their very nature and need no specific prohibition, as they are condemned under general moral law.

Other kinds of worship, though not inherently vicious, may still be forbidden by divine precept—whether explicitly in Scripture or through some other form of divine revelation—as being inconsistent with God's will, order, or appointed means of worship.

§3. Of the Rule that Limits the Kinds of Worship

For *natural worship*, the law of nature is the rule that limits and governs all its forms. But in *positive worship*—that is, all acts of worship that are not dictated by the natural law, but rest upon God's free determination—the kinds of worship must either be limited by divine institution or be left to human discretion.

It is universally acknowledged, by all who receive the Scriptures as the Word of God, that many kinds of positive worship have been divinely instituted. Likewise, it is plainly evident to anyone who observes the religious practices of the world, that many other kinds have been introduced by human invention. The question, then, is whether those acts of worship which arise from human choice are lawful, and whether they may lawfully be mingled with those which are divinely instituted.

To suppose that all kinds of positive worship should be left to human discretion is, in itself, *contrary to reason*. Man, by nature, is darkened in his understanding of divine things, inclined to error even in his best intentions, and prone to devise what is improper or unworthy in the service of God. Much more is this evident when we consider man's innate tendency toward superstition and presumptuous innovation in matters of worship.

And in fact, God has not left the matter to man's invention. Instead, he has expressly appointed the worship he requires in every age, knowing *best* what honors him and suits his divine nature.

It is also clear by reason that God, in instituting certain acts of worship, has made sufficient provision for his own glory, in a manner that suits the end and purpose of those ordinances. Therefore, for man to replace one of God's ordinances with another of his own making—though of the same nature and for the same purpose—or to add humanly devised ordinances as supplements, whether they be deemed necessary or merely helpful, is to presume upon God's wisdom and diminish the sufficiency of what he has ordained.

Such actions necessarily undermine the authority and perfection of *divine worship*. Consequently, it must be concluded that certain ordinances of divine worship are not subject to human discretion. Men may neither change them nor add to them others of like kind and purpose, even if only under the pretense of usefulness or spiritual benefit. Such additions—when offered as necessary or helpful supplements—are, in effect, violations of God's will.

This conclusion is supported by the express words of Scripture: "Ye shall not add unto the word which I command you, neither shall ye diminish ought from it," (Deuteronomy 4:2); and again, "What thing soever I command you, observe to do it: thou shalt not add thereto, nor diminish from it," (Deuteronomy 12:32). These verses prohibit not only additions to the written rule itself, but also the doing of anything beyond what the rule requires. The precept is not merely to keep the rule intact, but to do only what is commanded in it. While these laws directly forbid the mixing of heathen rituals with God's ordinances, they also plainly forbid any additions to divine worship by man, even if those additions are sincerely intended.

§4. What of Divine Worship May Not be Devised or Instituted by Man

Now let us consider what kinds of religious observances God has reserved to His own authority, and which are therefore forbidden to be devised or instituted by man.

First, anything that shares the same nature or purpose as those ordinances which God has already appointed for the universal Church until the end of the world may not be invented by man. For example, it would be unlawful to add another weekly holy day for the same spiritual purpose as the Lord's Day, or to create a new ordinance that parallels the sacraments of the covenant of grace.

Some argue that it is impossible for man to create a true sacrament of the covenant of grace, and therefore no man-made ordinance should be rejected on that basis. While it is true that only God can establish a valid sacrament, man can still wrongly presume to create an ordinance that imitates the sacraments in nature, function, and purpose—even if such a thing has no real authority or effect. Likewise, man may invent forms of worship that imitate divine ordinances, though they lack God's sanction and are therefore unlawful and unfruitful.

Regarding the benefit or efficacy of ordinances, we must distinguish between something being suitable to be useful (if God were to approve it) and something being actually useful. Many man-made practices may seem capable of spiritual benefit in theory, but that does not mean they will *actually* bring blessing. The true benefit comes not from the suitability of the thing itself, but *from God's institution of it*. What God has not appointed, *He does not bless for supernatural ends*; and what *is not sanctified* by Him *is not effective*.

Though God binds Himself to seal His covenant only through His own appointed means, men may still arrogantly devise ordinances that pretend to convey God's grace—implying, falsely, that God is sealing something through them. This is a dangerous presumption.

Moreover, the sacraments not only seal God's grace to us, but also confirm our self-dedication to Him under the terms of the covenant. So, if man creates a ceremony of self-dedication on covenant terms, even without divine sanction, he has essentially constructed at least half a sacrament.

Second, man may not invent any new essential part of divine worship—something without which God's worship would be considered incomplete. Doing so would amount to inventing a new part of Christianity itself, thereby adding to the religion beyond what Christ, its Founder, has ordained.

It must be noted that changes to the incidental or outward aspects of worship—such as clothing or cultural expressions—do not alter the substance of religion, just as changing a man's clothes does not change the man himself.

Third, man may not institute any ordinance that is to be used universally and perpetually in the Church—if it is to be used at all. Instituting such a practice implies that God's ordinances are lacking and must be supplemented. It wrongly presumes that these additional ordinances are necessary. But if anything is reserved to the authority of Christ, the universal Lawgiver, it is the power to create laws or ordinances that are binding on all places and times.

Nevertheless, a voluntary, temporary religious practice—used privately by individuals or particular churches for specific purposes that are consistent with Scripture—may be lawful, provided it is not imposed as a rule or law upon the Church. In such cases, Christ's legislative authority is not infringed, because the practice is not claimed as a divine ordinance, but only as a discretionary and private act.

§5. What Things Pertaining to Divine Worship May be Devised or Instituted by Man

The Third Part: Superstition

The items mentioned in the previous section as forbidden refer to new ordinances of worship that are *set alongside* God's own institutions—ordinances which, in their very nature, purpose, and usage, claim a status equal to God's own commands and therefore suggest that His institutions are insufficient. These are prohibited.

However, there are man-made institutions that exist in subordination to God's institutions. These serve to regulate or order worship more conveniently, and they are not true additions because they do not share the same nature or purpose as divine ordinances. Such subordinate matters, when rightly handled, are lawful.

All such forms or modes of worship that are required in general but not prescribed in particular (*i.e.*, where something must be done in some manner, but no specific manner is divinely appointed) are left to human decision.

That human determination must be governed by the general rules of God's Word—chiefly these two: (1) that everything be done for the purpose of edification, and not for harm; and (2) that all things be done decently and in order (cf. 1 Corinthians 14:26, 40). These rules are explicitly stated in Scripture and also follow from natural law.

These matters are neither essential nor integral parts of divine worship. If they are ever called "parts," it is only because they visibly express reverence toward God, and thus are accidental parts—such as the act of removing one's hat during prayer, which is a gesture of respect, and so is a form of worship only to that degree.

In this context, the term "accidental worship" is acceptable—not because these actions have no connection at all to worship, but because they are not essential or necessary parts of religion. Divine worship, as a category, includes a variety of expressions that differ in degree and importance. These subordinate or circumstantial actions participate in worship in the lowest degree. For example, removing one's hat is a gesture of honor and only as such has any religious significance.

These *accidental* elements are usually not performed in isolation but accompany more significant acts of external worship. Still, one might ask whether such gestures (e.g., bowing, kneeling, removing shoes) can themselves be acts of worship apart from any other act. For instance, when Moses removed his shoes before the burning bush, was that gesture an act of worship on its own, or merely a circumstance of another act? Even if it stands alone, such a gesture still belongs to the lowest category of accidental or circumstantial worship.

It seems that when the Lord told Moses to take off his shoes, He was not giving a new command of worship, but rather reminding Moses of what was already required, given the sacredness of the moment. Moses simply hadn't realized the occasion until God pointed it out.

Whatever custom or natural propriety makes a gesture or action reverent—such that omitting it would be disrespectful—ought to be included in worship under God's general commands. This is not an addition to God's law, but a lawful application of general principles to specific cases, which the law itself allows.

These are changeable matters—what is appropriate in one place or time may not be in another. Therefore, they are not suited to become universal laws, but are to be judged by prudence under the broader guidance of Scripture.

It should also be noted that those matters left to human decision must be necessary in general—not things that are useless or frivolous. A superior authority should not establish practices that, though not evil in themselves, are superfluous. Yet, a subordinate may sometimes lawfully go along with such things—not because they are binding in themselves, but to avoid trouble or show respect.

Also note: even among matters necessary in general, the one in authority must not impose a specific practice that, though not sinful in itself, is likely to cause harm or lead to evil, especially if there is a safer and equally suitable alternative. Yet the one under authority may choose to comply if refusing would cause greater harm than obeying.

§6. Concerning the Lawfulness of Significant Ceremonies in Divine Worship

By a *ceremony*, I mean an outward rite used in or around the worship of God. By *significant ceremonies*, I mean such rites used in divine worship that signify some substantial point of religion.

There is no dispute over outward actions that naturally or by common usage express reverence of the heart—such as kneeling, lifting the eyes and hands toward heaven as a token of devotion to the God of heaven, or removing one's hat in prayer (*cf.* Psalm 123:1; Exodus 9:29). But the question lies with those actions which signify, solely by the force of official institution or private, arbitrary intention. These acts, though they may have some natural suitability to signify religious truths, do not actually signify anything except by intentional assignment.

It is generally accepted that significant ceremonies in taking an oath may be lawfully used—not only those that naturally signify something, such as lifting up the hand to heaven (Genesis 14:22), but also those that signify by institution, like placing a hand on a book or kissing it. Though the goal of an oath may relate to civil matters, such as the resolution of a dispute, the *form* of the oath is divine worship (Hebrews 6:16). These ceremonies express the external part of the oath and signify by virtue of institutional assignment.

Words signify meaning by common usage and retain the same meaning inside and outside religious contexts. Therefore, the argument from their lawfulness as signs of worship to the lawfulness of instituted signs may be subject to challenge. Nevertheless, it may be said that instituted signs, once received and repeated soon become as customary and as intelligible as words.

In ancient times, Christians dwelling among pagans might lawfully have worn or displayed the symbol of the cross to identify themselves as Christians—meaning no more than if they had said aloud, "We belong to Christ" (Acts 11:26). But this was not an act of divine worship, only a communicative or declarative sign towards men.

I offer, with due acknowledgment of my limitations, my judgment in this matter: God has permitted words to be used as signs to express acts of divine worship, but I do not find that He has permitted words only while forbidding gestures or bodily actions for this same purpose. A mute person must express internal worship through gestures or actions, or else he cannot externally worship God at all. If signs of devotion with customary meaning are lawful, I do not see why signs of instituted meaning would be unlawful—especially if they come to be as commonly understood as those signs which arose without formal institution.

If instituted signs of general devotion are permitted, I find no reason why signs of a particular aspect of devotion or a doctrinal mystery should be forbidden.

I have more confidence in the lawfulness of rites and ceremonies used only in place of spoken words than in those that are added to words, in order to give them more solemn confirmation—like seals affixed to writings, or covenantal symbols added to verbal contracts (*cf.* Genesis 17:11). Nevertheless, those aforementioned oath-taking ceremonies appear to be additions to the words, meant to ratify the vow with greater solemnity. It makes no difference whether the words are read aloud by another or spoken directly by the person swearing, for in either case they are his words.

Also, I am more confident in the lawfulness of significant ceremonies that arise from private, personal intention than in those formally instituted by authority. I likewise find occasional and present-tense use (*pro hic & nunc*) more acceptable than stated or permanent use.

Moreover, I believe significant ceremonies in divine worship are prone to degenerate into superstition. When they are multiplied, they burden religion like useless baggage. They form a system of worship more reminiscent of the Mosaic form than the evangelical, which prioritizes spiritual worship (John 4:23–24; Colossians 2:20–23).

I also believe that significant ceremonies are not *necessary in kind* (*in genere*), unlike those things God has permitted human authorities to determine. Therefore, they ought not to be instituted or imposed in ordinary public worship.

I hold that Christ has instituted all stated ordinances of positive worship that are necessary for the universal church, and so additional rites of the same kind must not be devised by men (Matthew 28:20).

If there are any significant ceremonies truly necessary for some portion of the universal Church due to specific times and places, there seems a more legitimate argument for their institution within those contexts. However, the controversial ceremonies now among us appear to claim necessity for the whole Church across all times—if indeed they claim to be necessary at all.

Significant ceremonies of the same nature and purpose as Christ's perpetual ordinances for His Church may not be invented or instituted by man—particularly those that serve as symbols of the Covenant of Grace or of Christian identity (Galatians 5:2–4).

In cases where sober Christians differ in judgment, rulers ought to be cautious in imposing such ceremonies. They should not stretch the consciences of their subjects to comply with rites that would infringe on God's prerogative in the soul (Romans 14:5–6; 2 Corinthians 1:24).

If rulers command something beyond the limits of their authority—i.e., something not necessary in kind—then unless the thing commanded is intrinsically evil or brings about greater harm in its observance than in its omission, subjects may lawfully comply. Yet this is not *formal obedience*, but a temporary compliance for the sake of peace and to avoid greater evil (1 Corinthians 10:23–24).

§7. Concerning bowing at the Name of Jesus

It is reasonably assumed that in this practice, it is not the name itself that is being worshipped, but rather the Person who bears the name. The spoken name is merely the occasion for adoring the Person of Christ.

There is nothing in reason or in Scripture that proves it is inherently wrong to show reverence to Christ by bowing the body or through another respectful gesture when His name, Jesus, is spoken.

However, to make this bowing a *fixed ordinance of worship* is an excess in religion—that is, superstition (though not of the most extreme kind)—for several reasons: it binds Christians to a bodily gesture that is neither necessary nor of great weight; it makes them overly attentive to external motion, which leans toward formality and distracts from the inward power and life of devotion; it also creates a distinction where God has made none, giving elevated honor to one name above others—such as Christ, God, Lord, or Jehovah—without a solid basis for doing so.

While the name is not itself the object of worship, it is still being given a level of prominence not afforded to the other divine names, without sufficient warrant.

Yet, if this bowing is so strictly required that significant trouble would arise from refusing it, then I judge it may be done—not as formal obedience, but to avoid greater harm. In such a case, it might also be wise to bow at the names Christ, God, or Lord as well.

The passage in Philippians 2:10, "That at the name of Jesus every knee should bow," is a figure of speech indicating subjection to Christ, and the same expression appears in Romans 14:11 and is taken from Isaiah 45:23, where it describes subjection to God.

§8. Concerning Kneeling in the Sacrament

As for kneeling during the Lord's Supper, the question here is not whether it is beneficial or should be required, but only whether it is lawful. I find no evidence against its lawfulness.

Among us, kneeling is not an act of adoring the elements, nor is it an affirmation of Christ's bodily presence. Rather, it is either a posture of prayer during the act, or a sign of the most humble and reverent reception of these pledges of divine grace—or both.

Still, considering that the disciples received it from the Lord's hand while seated at a table, the use of a table-gesture cannot reasonably be considered less proper or fitting.

§9. Concerning Wearing the Surplice

As for the surplice: wearing a garment of a particular color, shape, or style in divine worship is neither commanded nor forbidden by God. While such garments may be materially indifferent, their formal use may not be.

If the surplice is regarded as a holy garment, like the priestly vestments under the law, or if it is used with the belief that the minister becomes *more holy* or that the service is *more pleasing* to God by it, then it is superstitious. If it is treated as a symbol of sanctity, it may raise concern. However, a distinct ministerial garment—whether worn daily or only during public worship—I do not regard as superstitious or forbidden. Still, a garment not marked by superstition may yet be too flashy or too theatrical.

What defines the formal use or purpose of the surplice should be judged according to the stated intentions of those who command its use.

Regardless of the garment's meaning, I cannot approve of forcing it upon ministers and congregations where, because of deeply rooted aversion, it is seen as either offensive or absurd—even if such aversion is considered blameworthy. Wise rulers will often yield to the fixed reluctance of their inferiors in matters that are non-essential and of little weight, even if originally well-intended.

And just as I would not wear a fool's garment during worship at the command of a superior, so also I would not appear before a congregation in a robe that I knew they regarded as ridiculous as a fool's coat, even if it were their *own fault* to see it that way.

§10. Concerning the Ring in Matrimony

Since the marriage contract and union, though a divine ordinance, is not a part of divine worship, I no more doubt the lawfulness of using the ring as a sign of that contract than I would doubt the lawfulness of using any other sign to confirm human agreements.

§11. Concerning the Cross in Baptism

Some Nonconformists state that they do not object to the civil use of the *cross* in coins or banners. Others admit they would not rebuke the early Christians who used the sign of the cross purely as a professing signal to indicate to the heathen that they believed in Christ crucified. In truth, that use of the sign was not an act of worship but rather a way of informing others about their faith.

It seems lawful to signify—whether by words or by other signs—that we belong to Christ and are His devoted servants. After all, words themselves are simply *one kind of sign*.

The reasons for scrupling the sign of the cross in baptism include the following:

It is not merely a circumstance but an ordinance of worship, and as such, it carries as much significance as any external rite possibly can.

Being a solemn and fixed symbolic sign of a divine mystery, and being devised by man, it belongs to the category of things which are not necessary in *genere* and therefore are not allowed to be determined and imposed by man, unlike those things which *are* necessary in *genere*.

Either it has the entire nature of a sacrament, or at least it contains part of what defines a sacrament.

It is argued that it qualifies as a sacrament because it is an outward and visible sign of inward and spiritual grace. The outward sign is the representation of the cross, the instrument of Christ's suffering; the inward grace is spiritual fortitude in the Christian warfare, as stated in the words of the Liturgy.

This sign intends to signify both the grace given to us by God and our duty to respond accordingly. Moreover, this sign is assigned a moral efficacy like that of a sacrament—it is said to work grace by teaching and stirring us to spiritual combat and by reminding us of Christ crucified. It also claims to signify and seal our union with Christ and our status as Christians. According to the Liturgy: *"We receive this child into the congregation of Christ's flock and do sign him... in token..."*

To the claim that no rite can be a sacrament unless instituted by God (see §4), the response is that although only God can institute a true sacrament, men may devise something with the same nature and intention, though it lacks divine sanction. And while those who impose the sign of the cross deny that it is a sacrament, if they define and use it in a way consistent with the form and nature of a sacrament, then in fact they have made it one—whether or not they admit it.

Even if we do not grant that it has the full and complete nature of a sacrament, there is undeniably one essential element of a sacrament in it: it functions as an engaging sign from us in the covenant. For we use it as a token of our engagement to Christ crucified—our Captain and Redeemer—by His cross, and of our commitment to live as His soldiers and servants to the end of our days.

Just as baptism dedicates one to Christ, so does the sign of the cross, according to the words of the Canon: *"It is an honourable badge whereby the party baptized is dedicated to the service of Him that died on the cross."* Thus, it contains at least part of what is essential to a sacrament, and shares in its nature to that extent.

Additionally, it seems to be of the same kind and nature as those ordinances which, according to the reasons laid out in §3, §4, and §5, Christ our Lawgiver has reserved *exclusively* to Himself.

§12. Concerning Holy-days

That a portion of every day ought to be spent in religious exercises, and that entire days of humiliation and thanksgiving should be observed on special occasions, and that there may be annual commemorations of great mercies or judgments, is scarcely disputed.

I see no reason why it would not be lawful for a nation or a people to establish an annual commemoration of some eminent person sent by God as a great light among them—such as the first proclaimer of the Gospel or a chief restorer of true religion—like Luther among the Germans or Calvin among the French Protestants. For few blessings can be said to surpass such in national benefit (Isaiah 52:7).

Mr. R.B. states that, given the eminence of the apostolic ministry as a mercy, he sees no reason why the churches of subsequent ages might not observe an annual day in remembrance of Peter or Paul, and so on. However, regarding the lawfulness of separating a yearly day for the commemoration of Christ's nativity, circumcision, and similar events—which occurred in the days of the apostles and held the same significance then as now—he is hesitant to judge, saying he cannot prove such days to be lawful, yet finds no clear prohibition.

Still, he offers several reasons for doubting their lawfulness:

The occasions for such days existed in the time of the apostles, and if God had desired them to be observed, He could as easily and appropriately have instituted them through the apostles in Scripture, just as He did other like matters (2 Timothy 3:16–17).

If such observances were necessary, they would be equally necessary in all ages and for all parts of the catholic Church; thus, they would require a universal law. But since God gave no such command in Scripture, to claim necessity is to undermine the sufficiency of Scripture as the universal rule of faith and divine obedience (Deuteronomy 4:2).

God has already appointed one day—the Lord's Day—to serve all the intended purposes, for the resurrection includes all the redemptive works of Christ (Luke 24:1; Revelation 1:10).

The Fourth Commandment, being part of the Decalogue, is of such high authority that it is not for man to create another weekly holy day in like manner (Exodus 20:8–11).

He holds it clearly unlawful for any earthly power to appoint a weekly day to commemorate any element of redemption, as it would replicate what God has already done by ordaining another. This appears to him as a presumption of authority not given, and an implicit charge against Christ and the Holy Spirit, as though their work were insufficient (Galatians 4:10–11).

Likewise, I believe it is an unwarranted assumption of authority for any human power to make a day or time permanently and immovably holy—as if it were a continual offering to God, not only made holy by the duties performed in it, but also making those duties more acceptable by its own sanctity (Isaiah 1:13–14).

As for observing—much more for imposing the observation of—holy days of merely human institution, one must consider not only what is lawful, but also what is expedient (1 Corinthians 10:23). It is as easy to err by excess as by neglect in instituting set times and days appointed for divine worship.

§13. Concerning a Liturgy

Any particular form—whether fixed or spontaneous—is not essential to prayer, but only pertains to its outward mode or expression, and relates to it not as a holy action specifically, but simply as an action. And since no action can be carried out except by some definite method, this sacred action must also take on *some shape* in its performance (John 4:24).

Neither Scripture nor the nature of prayer itself has made a stated, fixed form necessary in and of itself, nor a wholly free, extemporaneous one; therefore, either may rightly be used according to circumstances and sound discretion. On one side, those who reject all set forms *entirely* are weak and unwise; on the other, those who reject every immediately conceived or non-prescribed form are overly opinionated. Both tendencies reveal an excessive devotion to party rather than to truth (1 Corinthians 1:12–13).

§14. Concerning Religious Austerities, as Acts or Matter of Divine Worship

Certain austerities are improper in their very kind—such as the cutting and lancing practiced by the prophets of Baal (1 Kings 18:28), the flagellations of the

Papists, or extreme disciplines pursued by some of the ancients, even if done with devout intentions: like living perpetually atop a pillar or standing sleepless for days. Other austerities are not unfit in kind, but are excessive in degree—such as disproportionate fasting or abasement. These are all to be rejected and fall outside our present inquiry.

The question is rather this: may proper and allowable austerities be regarded not only as helpful accompaniments, but as actual acts or material of divine worship?

The internal abasement of soul before God—true humiliation or self-prostration—is an act of inward worship (Psalm 51:17). And it seems reasonable that such austerities may lawfully be employed as direct and immediate signs of this inward humiliation, and thereby be counted acts of worship themselves. Whatever directly and immediately expresses inward worship becomes external worship. Thus, fasting and various abstinences may be viewed not only as appropriate accessories to worship and useful aids within it, but as worship themselves (Joel 2:12–13; Matthew 6:16–18).

However, vows binding a person to these otherwise lawful austerities for life or for an extended period are dangerous. They tend to ensnare the conscience (Ecclesiastes 5:4–5), and when a unique religious status is assigned to such practices—beyond what pertains to Christianity itself—they become superstitions and instances of will-worship (Colossians 2:20–23).

Other Works at Puritan Publications on Worship

5 Marks of a Biblical Church by C. Matthew McMahon

5 Marks of Biblical Commitment to the Visible Body of Christ by C. Matthew McMahon

A Biblical Response to Superstition, Will-Worship and the Christmas Holiday by Daniel Cawdrey (1588-1664)

A Christian's True Spiritual Worship to Jesus Christ by Stephen Charnock (1628-1680)

A Declaration of the Christian Sabbath by Robert Cleaver (d. 1613)

A Discourse on Church Discipline and Reformation by Daniel Cawdrey (1588-1664)

A Discourse on Covenant Theology and Infant Baptism by Cuthbert Sydenham (or Sidenham) (1622–1654)

A Discourse on Self-Examination by Nathaniel Vincent (1639-1697)

A Gospel-Ordinance Concerning the Singing of Scripture Psalms, Hymns and Spiritual Songs by Cuthbert Sydenham (1622–1654)

A Practical Guide to Primeval History by C. Matthew McMahon

A Treatise on the Lord's Supper by Henry Smith (1550–1591)

A Watchman Over Christ's Church by C. Matthew McMahon

Attending the Lord's Table by Henry Tozer (1602-1650)

Bah Humbug: How Christians Should Think About the Christmas Holiday by C. Matthew McMahon

Christ's Directives on the Nature of True Worship by Arthur Hildersham (1563-1631)

Christian Truths Necessary for Salvation by Nicholas Byfield (1579–1622)

Covenant Holiness and Infant Baptism by Thomas Blake (1597-1657)

Directions for Daily Holy Living by Daniel Burgess (1645-1713)

Family Reformation Promoted, and Other Works by Daniel Cawdrey (1588-1664)

Gospel Music: or the Singing of David's Psalms by Nathaniel Holmes (or Homes) D.D. (1599–1678)

Gospel Worship, or, The Right Manner of Sanctifying the name of God in General, in Hearing the Word, Receiving the Lord's Supper, and Prayer by Jeremiah Burroughs (1599-1646)

How to Hear the Preaching of God's Word with Profit by Stephen Egerton (1555–1621)

How to Serve God in Private and Public Worship by John Jackson (1600-1648)

Infant Baptism God's Ordinance by Michael Harrison (1640-1729)

Infant Baptism of Christ's Appointment by Samuel Petto (1624–1711)

Love to God by Thomas Tuke (d. 1657)

Practical Observations on the Lord's Supper by C. Matthew McMahon

Presumptive Regeneration, or, the Baptismal Regeneration of Elect Infants by Cornelius Burgess (1589-1665)

Divine Worship

Singing of Psalms a Gospel Ordinance by John Cotton (1585-1662)

Singing of Psalms the Duty of Christians by Thomas Ford (1598–1674)

Sparks of Divine Glory: A Practical Study of the Attributes of God by C. Matthew McMahon

The Christian's Charge Never to Offend God in Worship by John Forbes (1568-1634)

The Christian's Duty to Reject Christmas by Thomas Mockett (or Mocket) (1602-1670)

The Cursed Family, or the Evil of Neglecting Family Prayer by Thomas Risley (1630–1716)

The Difficulties of and Encouragements to a Reformation by Anthony Burgess (1600-1663) and C. Matthew McMahon

The Doctrine and Practice of Infant Baptism by John Brinsley (1600-1665)

The Excellent Name of God by Jeremiah Burroughs (1599-1646)

The Glory of Evangelical Worship by John Owen (1616-1683)

The Guard of the Tree of Life, a Discourse on the Sacraments by Samuel Bolton (1606-1654)

The Holy Eucharist, or, the Mystery of the Lord's Supper Briefly Explained by Thomas Watson (1620-1686)

The Lord's Voice Cries to the City: A Biblical Guide for Hearing the Word of God Preached by C. Matthew McMahon

The Nature and Method of Secret Prayer by Samuel Lee (1625-1691)

The Preacher's Charge and People's Duty by John Brinsley (1600-1665)

The Puritans on Exclusive Psalmody Edited by C. Matthew McMahon

The Simplicity of Holy Worship by John Wilson (1588–1667)

The True Psalmody by Various Reformed Ministers

The Use of Instruments of Music in Christian Corporate Worship Indefensible by James Begg, D.D.

True Worship and the Consequences of Idolatry by John Knox (1505-1572)

Vain Imaginations in the Worship of God by Jonathan Edwards et al.

www.ingramcontent.com/pod-product-compliance
Lightning Source LLC
Chambersburg PA
CBHW020857160426
43192CB00007B/965